**STARK**

# KLASSENARBEITEN

## Englisch 8. Klasse

Xenia Riedl

**mit MP3-CD**

**STARK**

**Bildnachweis**
Umschlag: © Johncarnemolla/Dreamstime.com
S. 35: © Miflippo/Dreamstime.com
S. 40: © Martti/Fotolia.com
S. 41  Schilder zu: Birdfeeding, Muir Woods, Underground Station © Paul Jenkinson
Notice © Ch. Bartholmai
Känguru-Schild © Ron Sumners/Dreamstime.com
S. 43  © Kurt Seebauer, lizenziert unter cc-by-sa-3.0. URL:
http://commons.wikimedia.org/wiki/File:Bayerischer_wald1.jpg
S. 52  © novikat/Fotolia.com
S. 55  © Michael Flippo/Fotolia.com
S. 60  © Wmj82/Dreamstime.com
S. 68  © Clive Goddard/Cartoonstock.com
S. 73  © David Kay/Dreamstime.com
S. 83, 85 © David Lehner/Dreamstime.com
S. 87, 89 © Diademimages/Dreamstime.com
S. 99  Yosemite von oben nach unten: © Xenia Riedl, © Mattlau16/Dreamstime.com
Everglades von oben nach unten: © Lunamarina/Dreamstime.com, © Xenia Riedl
S. 106 © Gemenacom/Dreamstime.com
S. 126 © Meister-Mini, lizenziert unter cc-by-sa-3.0. URL:
http://commons.wikimedia.org/wiki/File:Morris_Mini_Moke.jpg
S. 148 Mayflower © Suchan/Dreamstime.com
Jamestown woman © americanspirit/Dreamstime.com
S. 156 © Chris Madden/Cartoonstock.com
S. 162 © Georgios Kollidas/Fotolia.com
S. 166 Salzburg © A_Lein/Fotolia.com
Mozart © Giuseppe Cignaroli/visipix.com
S. 170 Tower Bridge © Bernhard Thürauf/pixelio.de
Harbour Bridge © Barbara Riescher
S. 171 © Louishenault/Dreamstime.com
S. 172 © Matthijs Rijken/www.sxc.hu
S. 176 © Costa007/Dreamstime.com

ISBN 978-3-86668-708-0

© 2014 by Stark Verlagsgesellschaft mbH & Co. KG
www.stark-verlag.de

Das Werk und alle seine Bestandteile sind urheberrechtlich geschützt. Jede vollständige oder teilweise Vervielfältigung, Verbreitung und Veröffentlichung bedarf der ausdrücklichen Genehmigung des Verlages.

# Inhalt

Vorwort

**Kurzgrammatik** ........................................................................... 1
**Besonderheiten einiger Wortarten** ............................................ 1
1 Adjektive und Adverbien – *Adjectives and Adverbs* ......................... 1
2 Pronomen – *Pronouns* .......................................................... 5
3 Präpositionen – *Prepositions* ................................................. 7
4 Modale Hilfsverben – *Modal Auxiliaries* .................................... 8
**Infinitiv oder Gerundium? – Die infiniten Verbformen** ............... 9
5 Infinitiv – *Infinitive* ............................................................. 9
6 Gerundium (*ing*-Form) – *Gerund* .......................................... 11
7 Infinitiv oder Gerundium? – *Infinitive or Gerund?* ......................... 12
8 Partizipien – *Participles* ...................................................... 13
**Bildung und Gebrauch der finiten Verbformen** .......................... 14
9 Zeiten – *Tenses* ................................................................. 14
10 Passiv – *Passive Voice* ........................................................ 21
**Der Satz im Englischen** ............................................................. 22
11 Wortstellung – *Word Order* .................................................. 22
12 Konditionalsätze – *Conditional Sentences* ................................. 23
13 Relativsätze – *Relative Clauses* .............................................. 25
14 Indirekte Rede – *Reported Speech* .......................................... 27
**Anhang** ...................................................................................... 29
15 Liste wichtiger unregelmäßiger Verben – *List of Irregular Verbs* ...... 29

**Tests** ......................................................................................... 31
Test 1: *Verb forms, English in use* .............................................. 31
Test 2: *Reading comprehension* ................................................. 35
Test 3: *Modal verbs* ................................................................. 40
Test 4: *Mediation* .................................................................... 43
Test 5: *Vocabulary, phrasal/prepositional verbs* ............................ 46
Test 6: *The passive, vocabulary* ................................................. 50
Test 7: *Listening comprehension* ................................................ 55
Test 8: *Reported speech, vocabulary* .......................................... 59
Test 9: *Listening comprehension* ................................................ 62
Test 10: *If-clauses (type I–III)* .................................................... 65
Test 11: *Analysing a cartoon* ..................................................... 68

Test 12: *Mind map* .................. 71
Test 13: *Mediation, comment* .................. 73
Test 14: *Verb forms (active/passive, use of tenses)* .................. 77
Test 15: *Listening comprehension* .................. 79
Test 16: *Relative clauses* .................. 83
Test 17: *Gerund after prepositions, mixed bag* .................. 87
Test 18: *Cloze test* .................. 91
Test 19: *Vocabulary ("false friends"/crossword puzzle)* .................. 93
Test 20: *Infinitive or gerund* .................. 97
Test 21: *Picture task* .................. 99
Test 22: *Writing an e-mail* .................. 101
Test 23: *Reading comprehension* .................. 103
Test 24: *Guided writing* .................. 106

**Klassenarbeiten** .................. **109**
Klassenarbeit 1: *Listening comprehension, vocabulary, grammar, mediation* .................. 109
Klassenarbeit 2: *Reading comprehension, text production, mediation* .................. 117
Klassenarbeit 3: *Listening comprehension, grammar, mediation* .................. 123
Klassenarbeit 4: *Reading comprehension, mixed grammar, text production* .................. 132
Klassenarbeit 5: *Listening comprehension, English in use, writing an e-mail* .................. 139
Klassenarbeit 6: *Mediation, grammar, creative writing* .................. 148
Klassenarbeit 7: *Listening comprehension, English in use, picture task* .................. 154
Klassenarbeit 8: *Reading comprehension, grammar, mediation* .................. 162
Klassenarbeit 9: *Oral exam – Presentation, photo task, role play* .................. 170
Klassenarbeit 10: *Oral exam – One-minute talk, photo task, role play* .................. 176

**MP3-CD**
Test 7: *A conversation at the tennis club* .................. Track 1
Test 9: *Moving to Toronto* .................. Track 2
Test 15: *Spider Woman – a Navajo legend* .................. Track 3
Klassenarbeit 1: *Teenagers at work* .................. Track 4
Klassenarbeit 3: *Winton Outback Festival* .................. Track 5
Klassenarbeit 5: *Britain's Got Talent* .................. Track 6
Klassenarbeit 7: *Protecting the environment* .................. Track 7

**Autorin:** Xenia Riedl

# Vorwort

Liebe Schülerin, lieber Schüler,

in diesem Buch findest du zahlreiche Aufgaben-Sets, mit denen du dich auf Tests und Klassenarbeiten im Fach Englisch vorbereiten kannst. Die Klassenarbeiten und Tests sind inhaltlich auf die Lehrplanthemen abgestimmt und die Aufgabenformen kennst du sicher aus dem Unterricht. Folgende Hinweise helfen dir bei der Arbeit mit dem Buch:

- Die den Tests und Klassenarbeiten vorangestellte **Kurzgrammatik** steht dir zum schnellen Nachschlagen bei grammatikalischen Schwierigkeiten zur Verfügung.
- Die Hörtexte zu den *listening comprehensions* findest du auf der beiliegenden **MP3-CD**.
- Vor den Tests und Klassenarbeiten steht immer eine **Zeitangabe**, die dir sagt, wie lange du für die Bearbeitung brauchen darfst. Trainiere am besten mit den vorgegebenen Zeiten, damit du dich an das Arbeitstempo gewöhnst und bei einem Test oder einer Klassenarbeit in der Schule nicht in Zeitnot gerätst. Natürlich kannst du auch nur einzelne Aufgaben bearbeiten. Verkürze die Arbeitszeit dann entsprechend.
- Damit du die Aufgaben selbstständig bearbeiten kannst, findest du nach jedem Aufgabenteil entsprechende **Lösungsvorschläge**. Hier stehen auch immer **nützliche Tipps und Hinweise**, die dir bei der Bearbeitung helfen. Probiere zunächst in jedem Fall die Aufgaben selbstständig zu lösen, bevor du dir die Hilfen anschaust.
- Oft siehst du anhand der Anzahl der Lücken, wie viele Punkte du für eine richtig ergänzte Lösung bekommst. Dann kannst du deine Punkte leicht zusammenrechnen und dein Ergebnis mit dem **Notenschlüssel** abgleichen. So lässt sich gut einschätzen, welche Note du erzielt hättest.
- Für die Textproduktion ist neben der Gesamtpunktzahl auch die Bepunktung der Teilbereiche Inhalt und Sprache angegeben. Für jeden sinnentstellenden Fehler, den du im sprachlichen Bereich machst, bzw. für jeden ausgelassenen Inhaltspunkt, solltest du einen Punkt von der Gesamtpunktzahl für diesen Teilbereich abziehen.

Wähle die Klassenarbeiten und Tests, die du vor einer Prüfung übst, nicht nur nach dem Thema aus, sondern auch nach den Kompetenzbereichen. In der nächsten Klassenarbeit kommt eine Mediation dran? Ihr habt im Unterricht die Bildung des Passivs durchgenommen? Dann löse zur Übung die entsprechenden Aufgaben dazu.

Viel Spaß beim Üben und viel Erfolg bei der nächsten Klassenarbeit!

Xenia Riedl

# Kurzgrammatik

## Besonderheiten einiger Wortarten

### 1 Adjektive und Adverbien – *Adjectives and Adverbs*
Bildung und Verwendung von Adverbien – *Formation and Use of Adverbs*

**Bildung**
Adjektiv + *-ly*      glad → gladly

Ausnahmen:
- *-y* am Wortende wird zu *-i*    easy → easily
  funny → funnily
- auf einen Konsonanten folgendes *-le* wird zu *-ly*    simple → simply
  probable → probably
- *-ic* am Wortende wird zu *-ically*    fantastic → fantastically

  Ausnahme: public → publicly

**Beachte:**
- Unregelmäßig gebildet wird:    good → well
- Endet das Adjektiv auf *-ly*, so kann kein Adverb gebildet werden; man verwendet deshalb:
  in a + Adjektiv + *manner/way*    friendly → in a friendly manner
- In einigen Fällen haben Adjektiv und Adverb dieselbe Form, z. B.:    daily, early, fast, hard, long, low, weekly, yearly
- Manche Adjektive bilden zwei Adverbformen, die sich in der Bedeutung unterscheiden, z. B.:

| Adj./Adv. | Adv. auf *-ly* |
|---|---|
| *hard* | *hardly* |
| schwierig, hart | kaum |
| *late* | *lately* |
| spät | neulich, kürzlich |
| *near* | *nearly* |
| nahe | beinahe |

The task is hard. (adjective)
*Die Aufgabe ist schwierig.*
She works hard. (adverb)
*Sie arbeitet hart.*
She hardly works. (adverb)
*Sie arbeitet kaum.*

**Verwendung**
Adverbien bestimmen
- Verben,

- Adjektive,

- andere Adverbien oder

- einen ganzen Satz
näher.

She <u>easily</u> <u>found</u> her brother in the crowd.
*Sie fand ihren Bruder leicht in der Menge.*
This band is <u>extremely</u> <u>famous</u>.
*Diese Band ist sehr berühmt.*
He walks <u>extremely</u> <u>quickly</u>.
*Er geht äußerst schnell.*
<u>Fortunately</u>, <u>nobody was hurt</u>.
*Glücklicherweise wurde niemand verletzt.*

**Beachte:**
Nach bestimmten Verben steht nicht das Adverb, sondern das Adjektiv:
- Verben, die einen **Zustand** ausdrücken, z. B.:
  | | |
  |---|---|
  | *to be* | sein |
  | *to become* | werden |
  | *to get* | werden |
  | *to seem* | scheinen |
  | *to stay* | bleiben |

- Verben der **Sinneswahrnehmung**, z. B.:
  | | |
  |---|---|
  | *to feel* | sich anfühlen |
  | *to look* | aussehen |
  | *to smell* | riechen |
  | *to sound* | sich anhören |
  | *to taste* | schmecken |

Everything <u>seems</u> <u>quiet</u>.
*Alles scheint ruhig zu sein.*

This dress <u>looks</u> <u>fantastic</u>!
*Dieses Kleid sieht toll aus!*

## Steigerung des Adjektivs – *Comparison of Adjectives*

**Bildung**
Man unterscheidet:
- Grundform/Positiv *(positive)*
- Komparativ *(comparative)*
- Superlativ *(superlative)*

Peter is <u>young</u>.
Jane is <u>younger</u>.
Paul is <u>the youngest</u>.

## Steigerung auf *-er, -est*
- einsilbige Adjektive

- zweisilbige Adjektive, die auf
 *-er, -le, -ow* oder *-y* enden

old, old<u>er</u>, old<u>est</u>
*alt, älter, am ältesten*

clever, clever<u>er</u>, clever<u>est</u>
*klug, klüger, am klügsten*

simp<u>ler</u>, simp<u>lest</u>
*einfach, einfacher, am einfachsten*

narrow, narrow<u>er</u>, narrow<u>est</u>
*eng, enger, am engsten*

funny, funn<u>ier</u>, funn<u>iest</u>
*lustig, lustiger, am lustigsten*

## Beachte:
- stummes *-e* am Wortende entfällt
- nach einem Konsonanten wird *-y* am Wortende zu *-i-*
- nach kurzem Vokal wird ein Konsonant am Wortende verdoppelt

simp<u>le</u>, simp<u>ler</u>, simp<u>lest</u>

funny, funn<u>ier</u>, funn<u>iest</u>

fit, fi<u>tt</u>er, fi<u>tt</u>est

## Steigerung mit *more ..., most ...*
- zweisilbige Adjektive, die nicht auf *-er, -le, -ow* oder *-y* enden

- Adjektive mit drei und mehr Silben

useful, <u>more</u> useful, <u>most</u> useful
*nützlich, nützlicher, am nützlichsten*

difficult, <u>more</u> difficult, <u>most</u> difficult
*schwierig, schwieriger, am schwierigsten*

## Unregelmäßige Steigerung
Die unregelmäßig gesteigerten Adjektive muss man auswendig lernen. Einige sind hier angegeben:

good, better, best
*gut, besser, am besten*

bad, worse, worst
*schlecht, schlechter, am schlechtesten*

many, more, most
*viele, mehr, am meisten*

much, more, most
*viel, mehr, am meisten*

little, less, least
*wenig, weniger, am wenigsten*

## Steigerungsformen im Satz – *Sentences with Comparisons*

Es gibt folgende Möglichkeiten, Steigerungen im Satz zu verwenden:

- **Positiv:** Zwei oder mehr Personen oder Sachen sind **gleich oder ungleich:** *(not) as* + Grundform des Adjektivs + *as*

  Anne is <u>as</u> <u>tall</u> <u>as</u> John (and Sue).
  *Anne ist genauso groß wie John (und Sue).*
  John is <u>not as</u> <u>tall</u> <u>as</u> Steve.
  *John ist nicht so groß wie Steve.*

- **Komparativ:** Zwei oder mehr Personen/Sachen sind **verschieden** (größer/besser …): Komparativform des Adjektivs + *than*

  Steve is <u>taller</u> <u>than</u> Anne.
  *Steve ist größer als Anne.*

- **Superlativ:** Eine Person oder Sache wird besonders hervorgehoben (der/die/das größte/beste …): *the* + Superlativform des Adjektivs

  Steve is <u>the</u> <u>tallest</u> boy in class.
  *Steve ist der größte Junge in der Klasse.*

## Steigerung des Adverbs – *Comparison of Adverbs*

Adverbien können wie Adjektive auch gesteigert werden.

- Adverbien auf *-ly* werden mit *more, most* bzw. mit *less, least* gesteigert.

  She talks <u>more</u> <u>quickly</u> than John.
  *Sie spricht schneller als John.*

- Adverbien, die dieselbe Form wie das Adjektiv haben, werden mit *-er, -est* gesteigert.

  | fast | – | fast<u>er</u> | – | fast<u>est</u> |
  | early | – | earl<u>ier</u> | – | earl<u>iest</u> |

- Manche Adverbien haben unregelmäßige Steigerungsformen, z. B.:

  | well | – | better | – | best |
  | badly | – | worse | – | worst |
  | little | – | less | – | least |
  | much | – | more | – | most |

## Die Stellung von Adverbien im Satz – *The Position of Adverbs*

Adverbien können verschiedene Positionen im Satz einnehmen:

- Am **Anfang des Satzes**, vor dem Subjekt *(front position)*

  <u>Tomorrow</u> he will be in London.
  *<u>Morgen</u> [betont] wird er in London sein.*
  <u>Unfortunately</u>, I can't come to the party.
  *<u>Leider</u> kann ich nicht zur Party kommen.*

- **Im Satz** *(mid position)*
  vor dem Vollverb,

  She <u>often</u> goes to school by bike.
  *Sie fährt <u>oft</u> mit dem Rad in die Schule.*

  nach *to be*,

  She is <u>already</u> at home.
  *Sie ist <u>schon</u> zu Hause.*

  nach dem ersten Hilfsverb.

  You can <u>even</u> go swimming there.
  *Man kann dort <u>sogar</u> schwimmen gehen.*

- Am **Ende des Satzes** *(end position)*
  Gibt es mehrere Adverbien am Satzende, so gilt die **Reihenfolge:**
  Art und Weise – Ort – Zeit
  *(manner – place – time)*

  He will be in London <u>tomorrow</u>.
  *Er wird <u>morgen</u> in London sein.*
  The snow melts <u>slowly</u> <u>in the mountains</u> <u>in springtime</u>.
  *Im Frühling schmilzt der Schnee langsam in den Bergen.*

## 2 Pronomen – *Pronouns*

### Possessivbegleiter / Possessivpronomen – *Possessive determiners / Possessive pronouns*

Possessivbegleiter *(possessive determiners)* und Possessivpronomen *(possessive pronouns)* verwendet man, um zu sagen, **wem etwas gehört**.
Possessivbegleiter stehen vor einem Substantiv, Possessivpronomen allein:

| Possessivbegleiter: | Possessivpronomen: | | |
|---|---|---|---|
| my | mine | This is my bike. | – This is mine. |
| your | yours | This is your bike. | – This is yours. |
| his/her/its | his/hers/– | This is her bike. | – This is hers. |
| our | ours | This is our bike. | – This is ours. |
| your | yours | This is your bike. | – This is yours. |
| their | theirs | This is their bike. | – This is theirs. |

**Reflexivpronomen – *Reflexive Pronouns***

Reflexivpronomen *(reflexive pronouns)* **beziehen sich auf das Subjekt** des Satzes **zurück**. Es handelt sich also um dieselbe Person:

| | |
|---|---|
| *myself* | I will buy myself a new car. |
| *yourself* | You will buy yourself a new car. |
| *himself / herself / itself* | He will buy himself a new car. |
| *ourselves* | We will buy ourselves a new car. |
| *yourselves* | You will buy yourselves a new car. |
| *themselves* | They will buy themselves a new car. |

**Beachte:**
- Einige Verben stehen ohne Reflexivpronomen, obwohl im Deutschen mit „mich, dich, sich etc." übersetzt wird.
- Einige Verben können sowohl mit einem Objekt als auch mit einem Reflexivpronomen verwendet werden. Dabei ändert sich die Bedeutung, z. B. bei *to control, to enjoy, to help, to occupy.*

I apologize …
*Ich entschuldige mich …*
He is hiding.
*Er versteckt sich.*
He is enjoying the party.
*Er genießt die Party.*
She is enjoying herself.
*Sie amüsiert sich.*
He is helping the child.
*Er hilft dem Kind.*
Help yourself!
*Bedienen Sie sich!*

## Reziprokes Pronomen – *Reciprocal Pronoun ("each other/one another")*

*each other/one another* ist unveränderlich. Es bezieht sich auf **zwei oder mehr Personen** und wird mit „sich (gegenseitig)/einander" übersetzt.

They looked at <u>each other</u> and laughed.
*Sie schauten sich (gegenseitig) an und lachten.*
*oder:*
*Sie schauten einander an und lachten.*

**Beachte:**
Einige Verben stehen ohne *each other*, obwohl im Deutschen mit „sich" übersetzt wird.

| | |
|---|---|
| to meet | *sich treffen* |
| to kiss | *sich küssen* |
| to fall in love | *sich verlieben* |

## 3 Präpositionen – *Prepositions*

Präpositionen *(prepositions)* drücken **räumliche, zeitliche oder andere Arten von Beziehungen** aus.

The ball is under the table.
He came home <u>after</u> six o'clock.

Die wichtigsten Präpositionen mit Beispielen für ihre Verwendung:

- *at*
  Ortsangabe: *at home*
  Zeitangabe: *at 3 p.m.*

  I'm <u>at home</u> now. *Ich bin jetzt zu Hause.*
  He arrived <u>at 3 p.m.</u> *Er kam um 15 Uhr an.*

- *by*
  Angabe des Mittels: *by bike*

  She went to work <u>by bike</u>.
  *Sie fuhr mit dem Rad zur Arbeit.*

  Angabe der Ursache: *by mistake*

  He did it <u>by mistake</u>.
  *Er hat es aus Versehen getan.*

  Zeitangabe: *by tomorrow*

  You will get the letter <u>by tomorrow</u>.
  *Du bekommst den Brief bis morgen.*

- *for*
  Zeitdauer: *for hours*

  We waited for the bus <u>for hours</u>.
  *Wir warteten stundenlang auf den Bus.*

- *from*
  Ortsangabe: *from Dublin*

  Ian is from <u>Dublin</u>.
  *Ian kommt aus Dublin.*

  Zeitangabe: *from nine to five*

  We work <u>from nine to five</u>.
  *Wir arbeiten von neun bis fünf Uhr.*

- *in*
  Ortsangabe: *in England*

  Zeitangabe: *in the morning*

- *of*
  Ortsangabe: *north of the city*

- *on*
  Ortsangabe: *on the left,*
  *on the floor*

  Zeitangabe: *on Monday*

- *to*
  Richtungsangabe: *to the left*

  Angabe des Ziels: *to London*

<u>In England</u>, they drive on the left.
*In England herrscht Linksverkehr.*

They woke up <u>in the morning</u>.
*Sie wachten am Morgen auf.*

The village lies <u>north of the city</u>.
*Das Dorf liegt nördlich der Stadt.*

<u>On the left</u> you see the London Eye.
*Links sehen Sie das London Eye.*

<u>On Monday</u> she will buy the tickets.
*(Am) Montag kauft sie die Karten.*

Please turn <u>to the left</u>.
*Bitte wenden Sie sich nach links.*

He goes <u>to London</u> every year.
*Er fährt jedes Jahr nach London.*

## 4 Modale Hilfsverben – *Modal Auxiliaries*

Zu den **modalen Hilfsverben** *(modal auxiliaries)* zählen z. B. *can, may* und *must*.

### Bildung

- Die modalen Hilfsverben haben für alle Personen **nur eine Form**: kein -*s* in der 3. Person Singular.

- Auf ein modales Hilfsverb folgt der **Infinitiv ohne** *to*.

- **Frage und Verneinung** werden nicht mit *do/did* umschrieben.

Die modalen Hilfsverben können nicht alle Zeiten bilden. Deshalb benötigt man **Ersatzformen** (können auch im Präsens verwendet werden).

I, you, he/she/it,
we, you, they } must

You <u>must</u> <u>listen</u> to my new song.
*Du musst dir mein neues Lied anhören.*

<u>Can</u> you help me, please?
*Kannst du mir bitte helfen?*

8

- *can* (können)
  Ersatzformen:
  *(to) be able to* (Fähigkeit),
  *(to) be allowed to* (Erlaubnis)

  I <u>can</u> sing. / I <u>was able to</u> sing.
  *Ich kann singen. / Ich konnte singen.*
  You <u>can't</u> go to the party. /
  I <u>wasn't allowed to</u> go to the party.
  *Du darfst nicht auf die Party gehen. /*
  *Ich durfte nicht auf die Party gehen.*

  **Beachte:** Im *simple past* und *conditional I* ist auch *could* möglich.

  When I was three, I <u>could</u> already ski.
  *Mit drei konnte ich schon Ski fahren.*

- *may* (dürfen) – sehr höflich
  Ersatzform: *(to) be allowed to*

  You <u>may</u> go home early. /
  You <u>were allowed to</u> go home early.
  *Du darfst/durftest früh nach Hause gehen.*

- *must* (müssen)
  Ersatzform: *(to) have to*

  He <u>must</u> be home by ten o'clock. /
  He <u>had to</u> be home by ten o'clock.
  *Er muss/musste um zehn Uhr zu*
  *Hause sein.*

  **Beachte:**
  *must not/mustn't* = „nicht dürfen"

  You <u>must not</u> eat all the cake.
  *Du darfst nicht den ganzen Kuchen essen.*

  „nicht müssen, nicht brauchen" =
  *not have to, needn't*

  You <u>don't have to</u> / <u>needn't</u> eat all the cake.
  *Du musst nicht den ganzen Kuchen essen. /*
  *Du brauchst nicht ... zu essen.*

# Infinitiv oder Gerundium? – Die infiniten Verbformen

## 5 Infinitiv – *Infinitive*

Der **Infinitiv** (Grundform des Verbs) **mit** *to* steht z. B. **nach**
- bestimmten **Verben**, z. B.:

| | |
|---|---|
| to decide | (sich) entscheiden, beschließen |
| to expect | erwarten |
| to hope | hoffen |
| to manage | schaffen |
| to plan | planen |
| to promise | versprechen |
| to want | wollen |

He <u>decided</u> to wait.
*Er beschloss zu warten.*

- bestimmten **Pronomen** *(something, anything)* und **Substantiven**, z. B.:
  | | |
  |---|---|
  | *idea* | Idee |
  | *plan* | Plan |
  | *wish* | Wunsch |

- bestimmten **Adjektiven** (auch in Verbindung mit *too/enough*) und deren Steigerungsformen, z. B.:
  | | |
  |---|---|
  | *certain* | sicher |
  | *difficult/hard* | schwer, schwierig |
  | *easy* | leicht |

- **Fragewörtern**, wie z. B. *what, where, which, who, when, how* und nach *whether*. Diese Konstruktion ersetzt eine indirekte Frage mit modalem Hilfsverb.

We haven't got anything to eat at home.
*Wir haben nichts zu essen zu Hause.*

It was her plan to visit him in May.
*Sie hatte vor, ihn im Mai zu besuchen.*

It was difficult to follow her.
*Es war schwer, ihr zu folgen.*

We knew where to find her. /
We knew where we would find her.
*Wir wussten, wo wir sie finden würden.*

---

Die Konstruktion **Objekt + Infinitiv** wird im Deutschen oft mit einem „dass"-Satz übersetzt. Sie steht z. B. nach

- bestimmten **Verben**, z. B.:
  | | |
  |---|---|
  | *to allow* | erlauben |
  | *to get* | veranlassen |
  | *to help* | helfen |
  | *to persuade* | überreden |

- **Verb + Präposition**, z. B.:
  | | |
  |---|---|
  | *to count on* | rechnen mit |
  | *to hope for* | hoffen auf |
  | *to wait for* | warten auf |

- **Adjektiv + Präposition**, z. B.:
  | | |
  |---|---|
  | *easy for* | leicht |
  | *necessary for* | notwendig |
  | *nice of* | nett |
  | *silly of* | dumm |

She allowed him to go to the cinema.
*Sie erlaubte ihm, dass er ins Kino geht./
... ins Kino zu gehen.*

She waited for him to call.
*Sie wartete darauf, dass er sie anrief.*

It is necessary for you to learn maths.
*Es ist notwendig, dass du Mathe lernst.*

- **Substantiv + Präposition**, z. B.:
  opportunity for    Gelegenheit
  idea for    Idee
  time for    Zeit

- einem **Adjektiv**, das durch *too* oder *enough* näher bestimmt wird.

Work experience is a good <u>opportunity for</u> you <u>to find out</u> which job suits you.
*Ein Praktikum ist eine gute Gelegenheit, herauszufinden, welcher Beruf zu dir passt.*

The box is <u>too</u> <u>heavy</u> <u>for me</u> <u>to carry</u>.
*Die Kiste ist mir zu schwer zum Tragen.*

The weather is <u>good</u> <u>enough</u> <u>for us</u> <u>to go</u> for a walk. *Das Wetter ist gut genug, dass wir spazieren gehen können.*

## 6 Gerundium (*ing*-Form) – Gerund

**Bildung**
Infinitiv + *-ing*

read → read<u>ing</u>

**Beachte:**
- stummes *-e* entfällt
- nach kurzem betontem Vokal: Schlusskonsonant verdoppelt
- *-ie* wird zu *-y*

write → writ<u>ing</u>
stop → sto<u>pp</u>ing
l<u>ie</u> → l<u>y</u>ing

**Verwendung**
Die *ing* Form steht nach bestimmten Ausdrücken und kann verschiedene Funktionen im Satz einnehmen, z. B.:

- als **Subjekt** des Satzes

- nach bestimmten **Verben** (als **Objekt** des Satzes), z. B.:
  to avoid    vermeiden
  to enjoy    genießen, gern tun
  to keep (on)    weitermachen
  to miss    vermissen
  to risk    riskieren
  to suggest    vorschlagen

<u>Skiing</u> is fun. *Skifahren macht Spaß.*

He <u>enjoys</u> <u>reading</u> comics.
*Er liest gerne Comics.*

You <u>risk</u> <u>losing</u> a friend.
*Du riskierst, einen Freund zu verlieren.*

- nach **Verb + Präposition**, z. B.:

| | | |
|---|---|---|
| *to agree with* | zustimmen | |
| *to believe in* | glauben an | |
| *to dream of* | träumen von | She dreams <u>of</u> <u>meeting</u> a star. |
| *to look forward to* | sich freuen auf | *Sie träumt davon, einen Star zu treffen.* |
| *to talk about* | sprechen über | |

- nach **Adjektiv + Präposition**, z. B.: *(to be)* ...

| | | |
|---|---|---|
| *afraid of* | sich fürchten vor | He is <u>afraid</u> <u>of</u> <u>losing</u> his job. |
| *famous for* | berühmt für | *Er hat Angst, seine Arbeit zu verlieren.* |
| *good/bad at* | gut/schlecht in | |
| *interested in* | interessiert an | |

- nach **Substantiv + Präposition**, z. B.:

| | | |
|---|---|---|
| *chance of* | Chance, Aussicht | Do you have a <u>chance</u> <u>of</u> getting the job? |
| *danger of* | Gefahr | *Hast du Aussicht, die Stelle zu bekommen?* |
| *reason for* | Grund | |
| *way of* | Art und Weise | |

- nach **Präpositionen** und **Konjunktionen der Zeit**, z. B.:

| | | |
|---|---|---|
| *after* | nachdem | |
| *before* | bevor | Before <u>leaving</u> the room he said goodbye. |
| *by* | indem, dadurch, dass | *Bevor er den Raum verließ, verabschiedete er sich.* |
| *in spite of* | trotz | |
| *instead of* | statt | |

## 7 Infinitiv oder Gerundium? – *Infinitive or Gerund?*

Einige Verben können sowohl **mit dem Infinitiv** als auch **mit der *ing*-Form** stehen, **ohne** dass sich die **Bedeutung ändert**, z. B.
*to love, to hate, to prefer, to start, to begin, to continue.*

I <u>hate</u> <u>getting</u> <u>up</u> early.
I <u>hate</u> <u>to get</u> <u>up</u> early.
*Ich hasse es, früh aufzustehen.*

# 8 Partizipien – *Participles*

## Partizip Präsens – *Present Participle*

**Bildung**
Infinitiv + -*ing*
Sonderformen: siehe *gerund*
(S. 11)

talk → talk<u>ing</u>

**Verwendung**
Das *present participle* verwendet man:
- zur Bildung der Verlaufsform *present progressive*,
- zur Bildung der Verlaufsform *past progressive*,
- zur Bildung der Verlaufsform *present perfect progressive*,
- wie ein Adjektiv, wenn es vor einem Substantiv steht.

Peter is <u>reading</u>.
*Peter liest (gerade).*
Peter was <u>reading</u> when I saw him.
*Peter las (gerade), als ich ihn sah.*
I have been <u>living</u> in Sydney for 5 years.
*Ich lebe seit 5 Jahren in Sydney.*
The village hasn't got <u>running</u> water.
*Das Dorf hat kein fließendes Wasser.*

## Partizip Perfekt – *Past Participle*

**Bildung**
Infinitiv + -*ed*

talk → talk<u>ed</u>

**Beachte:**
- stummes -*e* entfällt
- nach kurzem betontem Vokal wird der Schlusskonsonant verdoppelt
- -*y* wird zu -*ie*
- unregelmäßige Verben (siehe Liste, S. 29 f.)

liv<u>e</u> → liv<u>ed</u>
sto<u>p</u> → sto<u>pp</u>ed

cr<u>y</u> → cr<u>ie</u>d
be → been

### Verwendung

Das *past participle* verwendet man
- zur Bildung des *present perfect*,

  He hasn't <u>talked</u> to Tom yet.
  *Er hat noch nicht mit Tom gesprochen.*

- zur Bildung des *past perfect*,

  Before they went biking in France, they had <u>bought</u> new bikes.
  *Bevor sie nach Frankreich zum Radfahren gingen, hatten sie neue Fahrräder gekauft.*

- zur Bildung des Passivs,

  The fish was <u>eaten</u> by the cat.
  *Der Fisch wurde von der Katze gefressen.*

- wie ein Adjektiv, wenn es vor einem Substantiv steht.

  Peter has got a well-<u>paid</u> job.
  *Peter hat eine gut bezahlte Stelle.*

# Bildung und Gebrauch der finiten Verbformen

## 9 Zeiten – *Tenses*

### Simple Present

**Bildung**
Infinitiv, Ausnahme 3. Person Singular: Infinitiv + *-s*

stand   –   he/she/it stand<u>s</u>

**Beachte:**
- Bei Verben, die auf *-s, -sh, -ch, -x* und *-z* enden, wird in der 3. Person Singular *-es* angefügt.

  kiss   –   he/she/it kis<u>ses</u>
  ru<u>sh</u>   –   he/she/it rush<u>es</u>
  teach   –   he/she/it teach<u>es</u>
  fi<u>x</u>   –   he/she/it fix<u>es</u>

- Bei Verben, die auf Konsonant + *-y* enden, wird *-es* angefügt; *-y* wird zu *-i-*.

  car<u>ry</u>   –   he/she/it carr<u>ies</u>

**Bildung von Fragen im *simple present***
(Fragewort +) *do/does* + Subjekt + Infinitiv

<u>Where does he live</u>? /
<u>Does he live</u> in London?
*Wo lebt er? / Lebt er in London?*

**Beachte:**
Die Umschreibung mit *do/does* wird nicht verwendet,
- wenn nach dem Subjekt gefragt wird (mit *who, what, which*),

Who likes pizza?
*Wer mag Pizza?*
Which tree has more leaves?
*Welcher Baum hat mehr Blätter?*

- wenn die Frage mit *is/are* gebildet wird.

Are you happy?
*Bist du glücklich?*

**Bildung der Verneinung im** *simple present*
*don't/doesn't* + Infinitiv

He doesn't like football.
*Er mag Fußball nicht.*

**Verwendung**
Das *simple present* wird verwendet:
- bei Tätigkeiten, die man **gewohnheitsmäßig** oder häufig ausführt
Signalwörter: z. B. *always, often, never, every day, every morning, every afternoon*

Every morning John buys a newspaper.
*Jeden Morgen kauft John eine Zeitung.*

- bei **allgemeingültigen** Aussagen

London is a big city.
*London ist eine große Stadt.*

- bei **Zustandsverben:** Sie drücken Eigenschaften / Zustände von Personen und Dingen aus und stehen normalerweise nur in der *simple form*, z. B. *to hate, to know, to like*.

I like science-fiction films.
*Ich mag Science-Fiction-Filme.*

### *Present Progressive / Present Continuous*

**Bildung**
*am/is/are* + *present participle*

read → am/is/are reading

**Bildung von Fragen im *present progressive***
(Fragewort +) *am/is/are* + Subjekt
+ *present participle*

<u>Is</u> Peter <u>reading</u>? / <u>What</u> <u>is</u> <u>he</u> <u>reading</u>?
*Liest Peter gerade? / Was liest er?*

**Bildung der Verneinung im *present progressive***
*am not/isn't/aren't* + *present participle*

Peter <u>isn't</u> <u>reading</u>.
*Peter liest gerade nicht.*

**Verwendung**
Mit dem *present progressive* drückt man aus, dass etwas **gerade passiert** und **noch nicht abgeschlossen** ist. Es wird daher auch als **Verlaufsform** der Gegenwart bezeichnet.
Signalwörter: *at the moment, now*

At the moment, Peter <u>is drinking</u> a cup of tea.
*Im Augenblick trinkt Peter eine Tasse Tee.*
*[Er hat damit angefangen und noch nicht aufgehört.]*

## Simple Past

**Bildung**
Regelmäßige Verben: Infinitiv + *-ed*

walk → walk<u>ed</u>

**Beachte:**
- Stummes *-e* entfällt.
- Bei Verben, die auf Konsonant + *-y* enden, wird *-y* zu *-i-*.
- Nach kurzem betontem Vokal wird der Schlusskonsonant verdoppelt.
- Unregelmäßige Verben: siehe Liste S. 29 f.

hope → hop<u>ed</u>

carr<u>y</u> → carr<u>ied</u>

sto<u>p</u> → sto<u>pped</u>

be → was
have → had

**Bildung von Fragen im *simple past***
(Fragewort +) *did* + Subjekt + Infinitiv

(<u>Why</u>) <u>Did</u> <u>he</u> <u>look</u> out of the window?
*(Warum) Sah er aus dem Fenster?*

**Beachte:**
Die Umschreibung mit *did* wird nicht verwendet,
- wenn nach dem Subjekt gefragt wird (mit *who, what, which*),

- wenn die Frage mit *was/were* gebildet wird.

Who paid the bill?
*Wer zahlte die Rechnung?*

What happened to your friend?
*Was ist mit deinem Freund passiert?*

Were you happy?
*Warst du glücklich?*

**Bildung der Verneinung im** *simple past*
*didn't* + Infinitiv

He didn't call me.
*Er rief mich nicht an.*

**Verwendung**
Das *simple past* beschreibt Handlungen und Ereignisse, die **in der Vergangenheit passierten** und **bereits abgeschlossen** sind.
Signalwörter: z. B. *yesterday, last week/year, two years ago, in 2008*

Last week, he helped me with my homework.
*Letzte Woche half er mir bei meinen Hausaufgaben.*
[*Die Handlung fand in der letzten Woche statt, ist also abgeschlossen.*]

## Past Progressive/Past Continuous

**Bildung**
*was/were* + *present participle*

watch → was/were watching

**Verwendung**
Die **Verlaufsform** *past progressive* verwendet man, wenn **zu einem bestimmten Zeitpunkt** in der Vergangenheit eine **Handlung ablief**, bzw. wenn eine **Handlung** von einer anderen **unterbrochen** wurde.

Yesterday at 9 o'clock I was still sleeping.
*Gestern um 9 Uhr schlief ich noch.*
I was reading a book when Peter came into the room.
*Ich las (gerade) ein Buch, als Peter ins Zimmer kam.*

## Present Perfect (Simple)

**Bildung**
have/has + past participle

write → has/have written

**Verwendung**
Das *present perfect* verwendet man,
- wenn ein Vorgang **in der Vergangenheit begonnen** hat und **noch andauert**,

- wenn das Ergebnis einer vergangenen Handlung **Auswirkungen auf die Gegenwart** hat.

Signalwörter: z. B. *already, ever, just, how long, not ... yet, since, for*

He has lived in London since 2008.
*Er lebt seit 2008 in London.*
*[Er lebt jetzt immer noch in London.]*

I have just cleaned my car.
*Ich habe gerade mein Auto geputzt.*
*[Man sieht evtl. das saubere Auto.]*

Have you ever been to Dublin?
*Warst du schon jemals in Dublin?*

**Beachte:**
- *have/has* können zu *'ve/'s* verkürzt werden.

- Das *present perfect* wird oft mit *since* und *for* verwendet („seit").
  - *since* gibt einen **Zeitpunkt** an:

  - *for* gibt einen **Zeitraum** an:

He's given me his umbrella.
*Er hat mir seinen Regenschirm gegeben.*

Ron has lived in Sydney since 2007.
*Ron lebt seit 2007 in Sydney.*

Sally has lived in Berlin for five years.
*Sally lebt seit fünf Jahren in Berlin.*

## Present Perfect Progressive/Present Perfect Continuous

**Bildung**
have/has + been + present participle

write → has/have been writing

**Verwendung**
Die **Verlaufsform** *present perfect progressive* verwendet man, um die **Dauer einer Handlung** zu **betonen**, die in der Vergangenheit begonnen hat und noch andauert.

She has been sleeping for ten hours.
*Sie schläft seit zehn Stunden.*

## Past Perfect (Simple)

**Bildung**
*had + past participle*

write → had written

**Verwendung**
Die Vorvergangenheit *past perfect* verwendet man, wenn ein Vorgang in der Vergangenheit **vor einem anderen Vorgang in der Vergangenheit abgeschlossen** wurde.

He had bought a ticket before he took the train to Manchester.
*Er hatte eine Fahrkarte gekauft, bevor er den Zug nach Manchester nahm. [Beim Einsteigen war der Kauf abgeschlossen.]*

## Past Perfect Progressive / Past Perfect Continuous

**Bildung**
*had + been + present participle*

write → had been writing

**Verwendung**
Die **Verlaufsform** *past perfect progressive* verwendet man für **Handlungen**, die in der Vergangenheit **bis zu dem Zeitpunkt andauerten**, zu dem eine neue Handlung einsetzte.

She had been sleeping for ten hours when the doorbell rang.
*Sie hatte (seit) zehn Stunden geschlafen, als es an der Tür klingelte. [Das Schlafen dauerte bis zu dem Zeitpunkt an, als es an der Tür klingelte.]*

## Will-future

**Bildung**
*will + Infinitiv*

buy → will buy

**Bildung von Fragen im *will-future***
(Fragewort +) *will* + Subjekt + Infinitiv

What will you buy?
*Was wirst du kaufen?*

**Bildung der Verneinung im *will-future***
*won't* + Infinitiv

Why won't you come to our party?
*Warum kommst du nicht zu unserer Party?*

**Verwendung**
Das *will-future* verwendet man, wenn ein Vorgang **in der Zukunft stattfinden** wird:
- bei Vorhersagen oder Vermutungen,
- bei spontanen Entscheidungen.

Signalwörter: z. B. *tomorrow, next week, next Monday, next year, in three years, soon*

The weather will be fine tomorrow.
*Das Wetter wird morgen schön (sein).*
[doorbell] "I'll open the door."
*"Ich werde die Tür öffnen."*

## Going-to-future

**Bildung**
*am/is/are + going to* + Infinitiv

find → am/is/are going to find

**Verwendung**
Das *going-to-future* verwendet man, wenn man ausdrücken will:
- was man für die Zukunft **plant** oder **zu tun beabsichtigt**.

- dass ein **Ereignis bald eintreten wird**, da bestimmte **Anzeichen** vorhanden sind.

I am going to work in England this summer.
*Diesen Sommer werde ich in England arbeiten.*

Look at those clouds. It's going to rain soon.
*Schau dir diese Wolken an. Es wird bald regnen.*

## *Simple Present* zur Wiedergabe der Zukunft *(timetable future)*

**Verwendung**
Mit dem *simple present* wird ein zukünftiges Geschehen wiedergegeben, das **von außen festgelegt** wurde, z. B. Fahrpläne, Programme, Kalender.

The train leaves at 8.15 a.m.
*Der Zug fährt um 8.15 Uhr.*

The play ends at 10 p.m.
*Das Theaterstück endet um 22 Uhr.*

## 10 Passiv – *Passive Voice*

**Bildung**
Form von *(to) be* in der entsprechenden Zeitform + *past participle*

The bridge <u>was</u> <u>finished</u> in 1894.
*Die Brücke wurde 1894 fertiggestellt.*

**Zeitformen:**

- *simple present*
  *Aktiv:* Joe <u>buys</u> the milk.
  *Passiv:* The milk <u>is</u> <u>bought</u> by Joe.

- *simple past*
  *Aktiv:* Joe <u>bought</u> the milk.
  *Passiv:* The milk <u>was</u> <u>bought</u> by Joe.

- *present perfect*
  *Aktiv:* Joe <u>has</u> <u>bought</u> the milk.
  *Passiv:* The milk <u>has been</u> <u>bought</u> by Joe.

- *past perfect*
  *Aktiv:* Joe <u>had bought</u> the milk.
  *Passiv:* The milk <u>had been</u> <u>bought</u> by Joe.

- *will-future*
  *Aktiv:* Joe <u>will buy</u> the milk.
  *Passiv:* The milk <u>will be</u> <u>bought</u> by Joe.

- *conditional I*
  *Aktiv:* Joe <u>would buy</u> the milk.
  *Passiv:* The milk <u>would be</u> <u>bought</u> by Joe.

- *conditional II*
  *Aktiv:* Joe <u>would have</u> <u>bought</u> the milk.
  *Passiv:* The milk <u>would have been</u> <u>bought</u> by Joe.

**Aktiv → Passiv**

- Das Subjekt des Aktivsatzes wird zum Objekt des Passivsatzes. Es wird mit *by* angeschlossen.
- Das Objekt des Aktivsatzes wird zum Subjekt des Passivsatzes.
- Stehen im Aktiv **zwei Objekte**, lassen sich zwei verschiedene Passivsätze bilden. Ein Objekt wird zum Subjekt des Passivsatzes, das zweite bleibt Objekt.

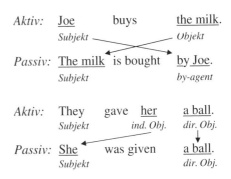

**Beachte:**
Das indirekte Objekt muss im Passivsatz mit *to* angeschlossen werden.

oder:

| | | | |
|---|---|---|---|
| *Aktiv:* | They | gave | her | a ball. |
| | *Subjekt* | | *ind. Obj.* | *dir. Obj.* |
| *Passiv:* | A ball | was given | | to her. |
| | *Subjekt* | | | *ind. Obj.* |

**Passiv → Aktiv**
- Der mit *by* angeschlossene Handelnde *(by-agent)* des Passivsatzes wird zum Subjekt des Aktivsatzes; *by* entfällt.
- Das Subjekt des Passivsatzes wird zum Objekt des Aktivsatzes.
- Fehlt im Passivsatz der *by-agent*, muss im Aktivsatz ein Handelnder als Subjekt ergänzt werden, z. B. *somebody, we, you, they.*

| | | | |
|---|---|---|---|
| *Passiv:* | The milk | is bought | by Joe. |
| | *Subjekt* | | *by-agent* |
| *Aktiv:* | Joe | buys | the milk. |
| | *Subjekt* | | *Objekt* |

| | | | |
|---|---|---|---|
| *Passiv:* | The match | was won. | |
| | *Subjekt* | | |
| *Aktiv:* | They | won | the match. |
| | *(ergänztes) Subjekt* | | *Objekt* |

# Der Satz im Englischen

## 11 Wortstellung – *Word Order*

Im Aussagesatz gilt die Wortstellung Subjekt – Prädikat – Objekt *(subject – verb – object):*

- Subjekt: Wer oder was tut etwas?
- Prädikat: Was wird getan?
- Objekt: Worauf/Auf wen bezieht sich die Tätigkeit?

Für die Position von Orts- und Zeitangaben vgl. S. 5

Cats catch mice.
*Katzen fangen Mäuse.*

# 12 Konditionalsätze – *Conditional Sentences*

Ein Konditionalsatz (Bedingungssatz) besteht aus zwei Teilen: einem Nebensatz *(if-clause)* und einem Hauptsatz *(main clause)*. Im **if**-Satz steht die **Bedingung** *(condition)*, unter der die im **Hauptsatz** genannte **Folge** eintritt. Man unterscheidet drei Arten von Konditionalsätzen:

## Konditionalsatz Typ I

### Bildung
- *if*-Satz (Bedingung): *simple present*
- Hauptsatz (Folge): *will-future*

If you <u>read</u> this book,
*Wenn du dieses Buch liest,*
you <u>will learn</u> a lot about music.
*erfährst du eine Menge über Musik.*

Der *if*-Satz kann auch nach dem Hauptsatz stehen. In diesem Fall entfällt das Komma:
- Hauptsatz: *will-future*
- *if*-Satz: *simple present*

You <u>will learn</u> a lot about music
*Du erfährst eine Menge über Musik,*
<u>if</u> you <u>read</u> this book.
*wenn du dieses Buch liest.*

Im Hauptsatz kann auch
- *can* + Infinitiv,

If you go to London, you <u>can</u> <u>see</u> Bob.
*Wenn du nach London fährst, kannst du Bob treffen.*

- *must* + Infinitiv,

If you go to London, you <u>must</u> <u>visit</u> me.
*Wenn du nach London fährst, musst du mich besuchen.*

- der Imperativ

stehen.

If it rains, <u>take</u> an umbrella.
*Wenn es regnet, nimm einen Schirm mit.*

**Verwendung**
Bedingungssätze vom Typ I verwendet man, wenn die **Bedingung erfüllbar** ist. Man gibt an, was unter bestimmten Bedingungen **geschieht** oder **geschehen kann**.

## Konditionalsatz Typ II

**Bildung**
- *if*-Satz (Bedingung): *simple past*
- Hauptsatz (Folge): *conditional I = would* + Infinitiv

If I went to London,
*Wenn ich nach London fahren würde,*
I would visit the Tower.
*würde ich mir den Tower ansehen.*

**Verwendung**
Bedingungssätze vom Typ II verwendet man, wenn die **Bedingung nur theoretisch erfüllt** werden kann oder **nicht erfüllbar** ist.

## Konditionalsatz Typ III

**Bildung**
- *if*-Satz (Bedingung): *past perfect*

- Hauptsatz (Folge): *conditional II = would + have + past participle*

If I had gone to London,
*Wenn ich nach London gefahren wäre,*
I would have visited the Tower.
*hätte ich mir den Tower angesehen.*

**Verwendung**
Bedingungssätze vom Typ III verwendet man, wenn sich die **Bedingung auf die Vergangenheit bezieht** und deshalb **nicht mehr erfüllbar** ist.

## 13 Relativsätze – *Relative Clauses*

Ein Relativsatz ist ein Nebensatz, der sich **auf eine Person oder Sache** im Hauptsatz **bezieht** und diese **näher beschreibt**:
- Hauptsatz:
- Relativsatz:

The boy who looks like Jane is her brother.
*Der Junge, der Jane ähnlich sieht, ist ihr Bruder.*
The boy ... is her brother.
... who looks like Jane ...

### Bildung
Haupt- und Nebensatz werden durch das Relativpronomen verbunden:
- *who* (Nominativ oder Akkusativ),

Peter, who lives in London, likes travelling.
*Peter, der in London lebt, reist gerne.*

*whose* (Genitiv) und

Sam, whose mother is an architect, is in my class.
*Sam, dessen Mutter Architektin ist, geht in meine Klasse.*

*whom* (Akkusativ) beziehen sich auf **Personen**,

Anne, whom/who I like very much, is French.
*Anne, die ich sehr mag, ist Französin.*

- *which* bezieht sich auf **Sachen**,

The film "Dark Moon", which we saw yesterday, was far too long.
*Der Film „Dark Moon", den wir gestern sahen, war viel zu lang.*

- *that* kann sich auf **Sachen** und auf **Personen** beziehen und wird nur verwendet, wenn die **Information** im Relativsatz **notwendig** ist, um den ganzen Satz zu verstehen.

The film that we saw last week was much better.
*Der Film, den wir letzte Woche sahen, war viel besser.*

**Verwendung**
Mithilfe von Relativpronomen kann man **zwei Sätze miteinander verbinden.**

London is England's biggest city.
London has about 7.2 million inhabitants.
*London ist Englands größte Stadt.*
*London hat etwa 7,2 Millionen Einwohner.*

London, which is England's biggest city, has about 7.2 million inhabitants.
*London, die größte Stadt Englands, hat etwa 7,2 Millionen Einwohner.*

**Beachte:**
Man unterscheidet zwei Arten von Relativsätzen:
- **Notwendige Relativsätze** *(defining relative clauses)* enthalten Informationen, die **für das Verständnis** des Satzes erforderlich sind.

  Hier kann das Relativpronomen entfallen, wenn es Objekt ist; man spricht dann auch von *contact clauses*.

- **Nicht notwendige Relativsätze** *(non-defining relative clauses)* enthalten **zusätzliche Informationen** zum Bezugswort, die für das Verständnis des Satzes nicht unbedingt notwendig sind. Dieser Typ von Relativsatz wird **mit Kommas** abgetrennt.

The man who is wearing a red shirt is Mike.
*Der Mann, der ein rotes Hemd trägt, ist Mike.*

The book (that) I bought yesterday is thrilling.
*Das Buch, das ich gestern gekauft habe, ist spannend.*

Sally, who went to a party yesterday, is very tired.
*Sally, die gestern auf einer Party war, ist sehr müde.*

# 14 Indirekte Rede – *Reported Speech*

Die indirekte Rede verwendet man, um **wiederzugeben, was ein anderer gesagt** oder **gefragt hat.**

**Bildung**
Um die indirekte Rede zu bilden, benötigt man ein **Einleitungsverb.**
Häufig verwendete Einleitungsverben sind:

to say, to tell, to add, to mention, to think, to ask, to want to know, to answer

In der indirekten Rede verändern sich die **Pronomen**, in bestimmten Fällen auch die **Zeiten** und die **Orts-** und **Zeitangaben.**

- Wie die Pronomen sich verändern, hängt vom jeweiligen **Kontext** ab.

| direkte Rede | indirekte Rede |
|---|---|
| Bob says to Jenny: "I like y<u>ou</u>." *Bob sagt zu Jenny: „Ich mag dich."* | Jenny tells Liz: "Bob says that he likes <u>me</u>." *Jenny erzählt Liz: „Bob sagt, dass er mich mag."* |
| Aber: | Jenny tells Liz that Bob likes <u>her</u>. *Jenny erzählt Liz, dass Bob sie mag.* |

- **Zeiten:**
  Keine Veränderung, wenn das Einleitungsverb im *simple present* oder im *present perfect* steht:

  In folgenden Fällen wird die Zeit der direkten Rede in der indirekten Rede **um eine Zeitstufe zurückversetzt**, wenn das **Einleitungsverb** im *simple past* steht:

| direkte Rede | indirekte Rede |
|---|---|
| Bob <u>says</u>, "I <u>love</u> dancing." *Bob sagt: „Ich tanze sehr gerne."* | Bob <u>says</u> (that) he <u>loves</u> dancing. *Bob sagt, er tanze sehr gerne.* |
| Bob <u>said</u>, "I <u>love</u> dancing." *Bob sagte: „Ich tanze sehr gerne."* | Bob <u>said</u> (that) he <u>loved</u> dancing. *Bob sagte, er tanze sehr gerne.* |

| | | | |
|---|---|---|---|
| *simple present* | → *simple past* | Joe: "I <u>like</u> it." | Joe said he <u>liked</u> it. |
| *simple past* | → *past perfect* | Joe: "I <u>liked</u> it." | Joe said he <u>had liked</u> it. |
| *present perfect* | → *past perfect* | Joe: "I'<u>ve liked</u> it." | Joe said he <u>had liked</u> it. |
| *will-future* | → *conditional I* | Joe: "I <u>will like</u> it." | Joe said he <u>would like</u> it. |

- **Zeitangaben** verändern sich, wenn der Bericht zu einem späteren Zeitpunkt erfolgt.
- Welche **Ortsangabe** verwendet wird, hängt davon ab, wo sich der Sprecher im Moment befindet.

| | | |
|---|---|---|
| now | → | then, at that time |
| today | → | that day, yesterday |
| yesterday | → | the day before |
| the day before yesterday | → | two days before |
| tomorrow | → | the following day |
| next week | → | the following week |
| here | → | there |

**Bildung der indirekten Frage**
Häufige Einleitungsverben für die indirekte Frage sind:

to ask, to want to know, to wonder

- **Fragewörter** bleiben in der indirekten Rede **erhalten**. Die **Umschreibung** mit *do/does/did* **entfällt** in der indirekten Frage.

Tom: "<u>When did</u> they arrive?"
*Tom: „Wann sind sie angekommen?"*

Tom asked <u>when</u> they had arrived.
*Tom fragte, wann sie angekommen seien.*

- Enthält die direkte Frage **kein Fragewort**, wird die indirekte Frage mit *whether* oder *if* eingeleitet:

Tom: "Are they staying at the hotel?"
*Tom: „Übernachten sie im Hotel?"*

Tom asked <u>if</u>/ <u>whether</u> they were staying at the hotel.
*Tom fragte, ob sie im Hotel übernachten.*

**Befehle/Aufforderungen in der indirekten Rede**
Häufige Einleitungsverben sind:

to tell, to order, to ask

In der indirekten Rede steht hier **Einleitungsverb + Objekt + *(not) to* + Infinitiv**.

Tom: "Stay here!"
*Tom: „Bleib hier!"*

Tom <u>asked me to stay</u> there.
*Tom bat mich, dazubleiben.*

# Anhang

## 15 Liste wichtiger unregelmäßiger Verben – *List of Irregular Verbs*

| Infinitive | Simple Past | Past Participle | *Deutsch* |
|---|---|---|---|
| be | was/were | been | *sein* |
| become | became | become | *werden* |
| begin | began | begun | *beginnen* |
| blow | blew | blown | *wehen/blasen* |
| break | broke | broken | *brechen* |
| bring | brought | brought | *bringen* |
| build | built | built | *bauen* |
| buy | bought | bought | *kaufen* |
| catch | caught | caught | *fangen* |
| choose | chose | chosen | *wählen* |
| come | came | come | *kommen* |
| cut | cut | cut | *schneiden* |
| do | did | done | *tun* |
| draw | drew | drawn | *zeichnen* |
| drink | drank | drunk | *trinken* |
| drive | drove | driven | *fahren* |
| eat | ate | eaten | *essen* |
| fall | fell | fallen | *fallen* |
| feed | fed | fed | *füttern* |
| feel | felt | felt | *fühlen* |
| find | found | found | *finden* |
| fly | flew | flown | *fliegen* |
| get | got | got | *bekommen* |
| give | gave | given | *geben* |
| go | went | gone | *gehen* |
| grow | grew | grown | *wachsen* |
| hang | hung | hung | *hängen* |
| have | had | had | *haben* |
| hear | heard | heard | *hören* |
| hit | hit | hit | *schlagen* |
| hold | held | held | *halten* |
| keep | kept | kept | *behalten* |
| know | knew | known | *wissen* |

| Infinitive | Simple Past | Past Participle | Deutsch |
|---|---|---|---|
| lay | laid | laid | *legen* |
| leave | left | left | *verlassen* |
| let | let | let | *lassen* |
| lie | lay | lain | *liegen* |
| lose | lost | lost | *verlieren* |
| make | made | made | *machen* |
| meet | met | met | *treffen* |
| pay | paid | paid | *bezahlen* |
| put | put | put | *stellen/setzen* |
| read | read | read | *lesen* |
| ring | rang | rung | *läuten/anrufen* |
| run | ran | run | *rennen* |
| say | said | said | *sagen* |
| see | saw | seen | *sehen* |
| sell | sold | sold | *verkaufen* |
| send | sent | sent | *schicken* |
| show | showed | shown | *zeigen* |
| sing | sang | sung | *singen* |
| sit | sat | sat | *sitzen* |
| sleep | slept | slept | *schlafen* |
| smell | smelt | smelt | *riechen* |
| speak | spoke | spoken | *sprechen* |
| spend | spent | spent | *ausgeben/ verbringen* |
| stand | stood | stood | *stehen* |
| steal | stole | stolen | *stehlen* |
| swim | swam | swum | *schwimmen* |
| take | took | taken | *nehmen* |
| teach | taught | taught | *lehren* |
| tell | told | told | *erzählen* |
| think | thought | thought | *denken* |
| throw | threw | thrown | *werfen* |
| understand | understood | understood | *verstehen* |
| wake | woke | woken | *aufwachen* |
| wear | wore | worn | *tragen* |
| win | won | won | *gewinnen* |
| write | wrote | written | *schreiben* |

# Test 1
## Schwerpunkte: *Verb forms, English in use*

**15 minutes**

**I   Spot the mistake**  (10 pts.)

Read Peter's e-mail to his new American e-friend from Florida.
There are 10 incorrect verb forms in the text.
Underline them and put them right.

---

An...: tom.brewer@mailz.com
Cc...:
Betreff: New e-pal

Dear Tom,

Thank you for your e-mail. My name is Peter and I'm 14 years old.
I haven't any brothers or sisters. My dog is called Snoopy.
Have you a pet?
We live in Hamburg since 2008. It's a big city, but I like it.
My school is OK. English is my favourite subject. I have spent my
holiday in England last year, but I was never to the US. If I would
have more money, I would go there on holiday.
Life in Florida must be great. Please tell me more about it. Are you
going to the beach every day? What hobbies have you?
What's your school like?
I must finish now because my mother waits for me. I hope you write
back soon.

Bye,
Peter

---

1 _____    2 _____
3 _____    4 _____
5 _____    6 _____
7 _____    8 _____
9 _____    10 _____

## II English in use (10 pts.)

Some weeks later Peter has to give a short talk about school in England and the USA. But there are some words that he does not know. During break, he asks you to help him fill in the gaps.
Change the German words into English to complete the sentences. If you do not know the word/phrase, try to paraphrase.

Children in England and the US start school at the age of five. First, they *(besuchen?)* _____ (1) *(Grundschule?)* _____ (2). From the age of 10, children in the US go on to *(weiterführende Schule?)* _____ (3). In England this kind of school is called comprehensive school. Both types of school provide secondary *(Erziehung?)* _____ (4) for all pupils. There are a number of *(Fächer?)* _____ (5) all children have to take, like English, Maths, *(Naturwissenschaft?)* _____ (6) and History, but in the US pupils have more choice. For example, creative writing, *(Kunst?)* _____ (7), Music and *(Sportunterricht?)* _____ (8) play an important role and there are many after-school clubs that offer activities like athletics, cheerleading or *(Theaterspiel?)* _____ (9). At the age of 16 English teenagers prepare for their GCSE *(Prüfungen?)* _____ (10), but some of them stay at school to take their A-levels two years later. Young Americans finish school at the age of 17 or 18.

| 1 | |
|---|---|
| 2 | |
| 3 | |
| 4 | |
| 5 | |
| 6 | |
| 7 | |
| 8 | |
| 9 | |
| 10 | |

# Solution

## I Spot the mistake

*Hinweis: Der Brief enthält 10 typische Fehlerquellen hinsichtlich der englischen Zeiten. Um sie zu umgehen, achte besonders auf die richtige Formenbildung. Signalwörter („last", „never" etc.) können dir dabei helfen. Einen Überblick über Bildung und Gebrauch der Zeiten im Englischen findest du auf den Seiten 14 bis 20 in der Kurzgrammatik.*

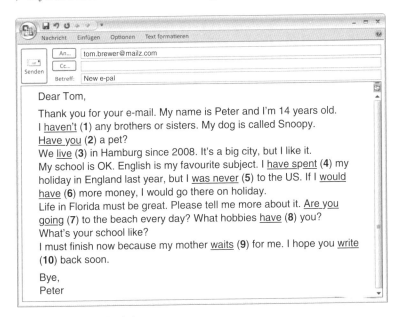

1  haven't got / don't have
2  Have you got / Do you have
3  have lived / have been living
4  spent
5  have never been
6  had
7  Do you go
8  do you have? / What are your hobbies?
9  is waiting
10 will write / 'll write

## II English in use

*Hinweis: Versuche, für alle Lücken einen geeigneten englischen Ausdruck zu finden. Wenn dir die Vokabel nicht einfällt, umschreibe das gesuchte Wort so genau wie möglich. Schreibe alle Wörter, die du nicht wusstest oder vielleicht nur falsch geschrieben hast, nochmals richtig in dein Vokabelheft, auf Karteikarten oder in ein Computerprogramm. So kannst du wichtige Vokabeln rund um das Themengebiet Schule besser im Gedächtnis behalten. Vielleicht hilft es dir auch, die in dieser Übung vorkommenden Wörter in einer Mindmap anzuordnen. Ein Beispiel für eine solche Darstellung findest du auf Seite 71 (Test 12).*

| 1 | go to / attend |
|---|---|
| 2 | primary school / elementary school / school for small children |
| 3 | high school |
| 4 | education |
| 5 | subjects |
| 6 | Science |
| 7 | Art |
| 8 | PE (physical education) |
| 9 | drama |
| 10 | exams / tests |

**Notenschlüssel:**

| 1 | 2 | 3 | 4 | 5 | 6 |
|---|---|---|---|---|---|
| 20–19 | 18–16 | 15–13 | 12–10 | 9–7 | 6–0 |

# Test 2
## Schwerpunkt: *Reading comprehension*

**20 minutes**

### Reading comprehension: Sports in the US

1 Sports play an important role in American society. Many people consider sports to be a very serious matter and are obsessed with winning and making money, while for others sport is a relaxing free-time activity.

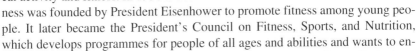

5 Team sports especially are extremely popular in the US. Millions of people watch games like baseball, basketball or football. Sports bring different classes and groups of society together and in this way contribute to racial and social integration.

10 American society has always stressed the need for physical activity and fitness. In 1956 a Council on Youth Fitness was founded by President Eisenhower to promote fitness among young people. It later became the President's Council on Fitness, Sports, and Nutrition, which develops programmes for people of all ages and abilities and wants to en-
15 courage Americans to lead a healthier life. The United States offers unlimited opportunities to do sport. Team sports have been popular since colonial times. Baseball, basketball and football arose from games brought to America by the first settlers in the 17th century and have grown into the most typical American kinds of sport, played and watched by millions of people.

20 Sports give teenagers the chance to get fit, to learn the value of fair play, to achieve goals and have fun. More than 50 percent of the boys and girls in high school are members of sports teams. Sports also play an important role in the everyday life at American colleges and universities. Many institutions offer sports scholarships to students who are both academically qualified and skilled at
25 a particular kind of sport. So students can play for a college team, "earning" the money they need for college education.

Different rituals have developed around sports competitions. The local high school football or basketball game represents the biggest event of the week for many communities across the US. Important competitions are accompanied by
30 parades and cheerleading shows and fans of university and professional football teams meet outside stadiums for a picnic lunch before kickoff. The Super Bowl, the championship game of the National Football League, is surrounded by shows featuring pop and rock stars, and many Americans celebrate it with parties in front of their TV sets.

*(364 words)*

**I  Vocabulary** (9 pts.)

**A  Give synonyms.**
1. to consider (l. 2): _____
2. goal (l. 21): _____

**B  Find the words belonging to the same word family.**
1. colonial (l. 16) – noun: _____
2. settler (l. 18) – verb: _____
3. value (l. 20) – adjective: _____

**C  Paraphrase the underlined expressions.**
1. "[(to) be] <u>extremely popular</u>" (l. 5):
   _____
   _____

2. "[(to) be] <u>academically qualified</u>" (l. 24):
   _____
   _____

**II  Comprehension**

1. Sum up why sports play a big role in US society. (6 pts.)
   _____
   _____
   _____
   _____
   _____
   _____
   _____

2. Explain why American politicians have always encouraged people to do sport. (4 pts.)
   _____
   _____
   _____
   _____
   _____

## III Beyond the text

1. Compare the attitudes towards sports in the US and Germany. Focus on **two aspects**. (4 pts.)

2. Describe what "sports scholarships" (l. 24) mean for American students. (6 pts.)

# Solution

## Reading comprehension: Sports in the US
### I Vocabulary

*Hinweis:* Wenn du Probleme mit Synonymen hast, schlage am besten in einem einsprachigen Wörterbuch die Bedeutung der Wörter nach und notiere dir die Synonyme. Bei Wörtern, die derselben Wortfamilie angehören, ist im Englischen sehr oft der Wortstamm gleich (z. B. „clean-" für „to clean", „cleaner" und „cleaning"). Versuche bei Paraphrasen die Begriffe mit einfachen Worten zu umschreiben. Überlege dir, wie du die Wortbedeutung auf Deutsch erklären würdest und übertrage deine Ideen dann ins Englische. Für jedes richtige Wort (A/B) erhältst du 1 Punkt, für jede Paraphrase (C) 2 Punkte.

**A Give synonyms.**
1. to believe/to think
2. aim

**B Find the words belonging to the same word family.**
1. colony/colonist
2. to settle
3. valuable

**C Paraphrase the underlined expressions.**
1. [(to) be] (very much) liked by everybody
2. [(to) have] (very) good marks/high grades at school or college

### II Comprehension

*Hinweis:* Lies den Text genau und markiere die Abschnitte, die für die Lösung der Verständnisaufgaben wichtig sind. Dann fällt es dir leichter, alle wichtigen Informationen im Blick zu behalten und die einzelnen Fragestellungen voneinander abzugrenzen. Achte darauf, bei den Antworten soweit wie möglich eigene Formulierungen zu verwenden.

1. Americans think that by participating in team sports you learn how to act fairly and work together with different kinds of people. So sports are supposed to improve the relationship between the races and social classes. Sports activities are also considered to be a lot of fun, improve your health and teach you how to achieve your aims in life.

2. As sports are considered to improve fitness and health, officials want everybody to practise some sport, not only young people or skilled athletes.

## III  Beyond the text

*Hinweis: In der ersten Aufgabe geht es darum, Informationen aus dem Text aufzugreifen (hier: den Stellenwert von Sport in den USA) und mit deinem eigenen Hintergrundwissen zu vergleichen (hier: der Rolle, die der Sport in Deutschland hat).*

*Für die zweite Aufgabe solltest du dich vor allem auf die Zeilen 23 bis 26 konzentrieren und über den Text hinaus denken. Überlege dir, welche Vorteile ein Sportstipendium für einen Studenten hat und welche Folgen es wohl hätte, wenn es diese Stipendien in den USA nicht gäbe.*

1. Possible aspects:
   - Sports teams play a more important role in American schools and universities than in Germany. The whole community is interested in their competitions and there are celebrations like shows, parties and parades all over the country when the Super Bowl takes place.
   - In the US, talented athletes get "sports scholarships" to pay for their college fees. In Germany, there is no such thing.

2. "Sports scholarships" mean that students who have a talent for a certain sport play in the college team and get financial help to pay for their college or university fees, so they do not have to do other jobs and can concentrate on their education and their sport.

## Notenschlüssel:

| 1 | 2 | 3 | 4 | 5 | 6 |
|---|---|---|---|---|---|
| 29–26 | 25–22 | 21–18 | 17–14 | 13–10 | 9–0 |

# Test 3
## Schwerpunkt: *Modal verbs*

**20 minutes**

**I  A trip to the San Diego Zoo** (8 pts.)

Fill in the missing modal verbs.

1. Last year Tom's class _____ *(müssen)* do a project on wild animals.

2. Of course they _____ *(nicht können)* go on a safari to Africa, but they _____ *(dürfen)* spend a day at the San Diego Zoo to study the animals there.

3. "_____ *(können)* we visit the Safari Park, too?" asked Jenny.

4. "No, I'm sorry, we won't have time to go there," Mr Brown answered. "But you _____ *(dürfen)* watch one of the animal shows."

5. John wanted to know if they _____ *(können)* take their cameras with them.

6. Mr Brown laughed. "Of course! You _____ *(müssen)* to take pictures for your presentation.

7. And you _____ *(nicht dürfen)* forget to bring the questionnaires I gave you yesterday."

## II Explain what the posters, signs etc. mean. (10 pts.)

Write sentences using suitable modal verbs.

1. _____

2. _____

3. _____

4. _____

5. _____

**Solution**

**I  A trip to the San Diego Zoo**

> *Hinweis:* Hier musst du jeweils auf den Sinn der Aussagen (Verpflichtung, Erlaubnis oder Fähigkeit) und die richtige Zeitform achten. Denke daran, dass manche Hilfsverben (z. B. „must" oder „mustn't") nicht einfach in die Vergangenheitsform gesetzt werden können, sondern eine Ersatzform benötigen. Wenn du dir bei der Bildung und Verwendung der Hilfsverben noch nicht so sicher bist, kannst du die Regeln auf Seite 8 und 9 nochmals nachschlagen.

1. Last year Tom's class **had to** do a project on wild animals.
2. Of course they **couldn't / weren't able to** go on a safari to Africa, but they **were allowed to** spend a day at the San Diego Zoo to study the animals there.
3. "**Can** we visit the Safari Park, too?" asked Jenny.
4. "No, I'm sorry, we won't have time to go there," Mr Brown answered. "But you **will / 'll be allowed to** watch one of the animal shows."
5. John wanted to know if they **could** take their cameras with them.
6. Mr Brown laughed. "Of course! You **will have to** take pictures for your presentation.
7. And you **mustn't** forget to bring the questionnaires I gave you yesterday."

**II  Explain what the posters, signs etc. mean.**

1. You need to be / must be quiet if you return late at night.
2. You can use the underground train from here.
3. You mustn't / are not allowed to smoke, ride a bike, have a picnic or bring your dog.
4. People mustn't / aren't allowed to feed the birds here.
5. You have to watch out for kangaroos.

**Notenschlüssel:**

| 1 | 2 | 3 | 4 | 5 | 6 |
|---|---|---|---|---|---|
| 18–17 | 16–15 | 14–12 | 11–9 | 8–6 | 5–0 |

# Test 4
## Schwerpunkt: *Mediation*

**15 minutes**

**Mediation: Visiting the Bavarian Forest National Park** (18 pts.)

You are visiting the Bavarian Forest National Park with Olivia, a friend from England. A park ranger is telling you some interesting facts about the park. Olivia cannot understand all the German explanations and asks you to interpret.
Only explain **the most important information** to her in English.

RANGER: Als erster deutscher Nationalpark wurde am 7. Oktober 1970 unser Park im Bayerischen Wald eröffnet. Er ist der größte deutsche Waldnationalpark. Nach einem Sturm 1983 wurden die zerstörten Flächen nicht aufgeforstet, sondern durften sich natürlich entwickeln und bilden nun einen undurchdringlichen Urwald. Windwurf, Schneebruch, Rotwild und Borkenkäfer veränderten den Wald über die Jahre.

YOU: _____

RANGER: Im Besucherzentrum finden Sie eine Informationstheke mit Plänen und Prospekten und ein kleines Museum mit wechselnden Ausstellungen. Außerdem gibt es ein Kino (es bietet auch eine englische Diashow), ein Café, eine Gaststätte und einen Laden, wo man Andenken und Geschenke kaufen kann. Gleich nebenan ist ein Naturgarten mit 700 Wildpflanzenarten und ein Baumwipfelpfad.

YOU: _____

RANGER: Sie können den Park auf bequemen Fußwegen erkunden und verschiedene Tiere, z. B. Hirsche, Bären und Wölfe, in Gehegen beobachten. Bitte bleiben Sie auf den markierten Wegen! Achten Sie zu ihrer eigenen Sicherheit auf herabstürzende Äste und verlassen Sie den Wald bei stürmischem Wind! Stören Sie die Tiere nicht, pflücken Sie keine Pflanzen und hinterlassen Sie keinen Abfall!

YOU: _____

# Solution

## Mediation: Visiting the Bavarian Forest National Park

*✐ **Hinweis:** Du musst die Erklärungen zum Nationalpark nicht wörtlich übersetzen,*
*✐ dafür sind sie zu umfangreich und enthalten Begriffe, die du noch nicht überset-*
*✐ zen kannst. Gib nur die wichtigsten Inhalte wieder. Unbekannte Begriffe kannst*
*✐ du umschreiben oder durch Oberbegriffe ersetzen (z. B. ist Blume der Oberbe-*
*✐ griff von Tulpe und Nelke). Für jeden fehlerfreien Abschnitt erhältst du 6 Punkte.*

RANGER: Als erster deutscher Nationalpark wurde am 7. Oktober 1970 unser Park im Bayerischen Wald eröffnet. Er ist der größte deutsche Waldnationalpark. Nach einem Sturm 1983 wurden die zerstörten Flächen nicht aufgeforstet, sondern durften sich natürlich entwickeln und bilden nun einen undurchdringlichen Urwald. Windwurf, Schneebruch, Rotwild und Borkenkäfer veränderten den Wald über die Jahre.

YOU: The park was opened on October 7, 1970. It is the largest German national park. After a huge storm in 1983 the destroyed parts of the forest were able to develop freely. Storms, snow, deer and insects have changed the park since then.

RANGER: Im Besucherzentrum finden Sie eine Informationstheke mit Plänen und Propekten und ein kleines Museum mit wechselnden Ausstellungen. Außerdem gibt es ein Kino (es bietet auch eine englische Diashow), ein Café, eine Gaststätte und einen Laden, wo man Andenken und Geschenke kaufen kann. Gleich nebenan ist ein Naturgarten mit 700 Wildpflanzenarten und ein Baumwipfelpfad.

YOU: In the Visitor Centre there is an information desk and a small museum. There is a cinema with an English show, a cafeteria and a shop, where you can buy souvenirs and presents. Next to the Visitor Centre there is a garden with 700 wild plants/flowers and also a nice walk close to the trees high above the ground.

RANGER: Sie können den Park auf bequemen Fußwegen erkunden und verschiedene Tiere, z. B. Hirsche, Bären und Wölfe, in Gehegen beobachten. Bitte bleiben Sie auf den markierten Wegen! Achten Sie zu ihrer eigenen Sicherheit auf herabstürzende Äste und verlassen Sie den Wald bei stürmischem Wind! Stören Sie die Tiere nicht, pflücken Sie keine Pflanzen und hinterlassen Sie keinen Abfall!

YOU: You can walk/hike through the park and watch animals like deer, bears and wolves behind fences, but you mustn't leave the tracks/paths. You must watch out for falling branches and leave the forest if there is a storm. You aren't allowed to disturb the animals, pick flowers or leave rubbish in the park.

## Notenschlüssel:

| 1 | 2 | 3 | 4 | 5 | 6 |
|---|---|---|---|---|---|
| 18–17 | 16–15 | 14–12 | 11–9 | 8–6 | 5–0 |

# Test 5
## Schwerpunkte: *Vocabulary, phrasal/prepositional verbs*

**15 minutes**

**I  Find a synonym for each word underlined.** (6 pts.)

1. John could not see the tree anymore because of the <u>mist</u>.

2. Finally, it became <u>clear</u> to him that he had lost his way.

3. John was <u>mad</u> with anger.

4. "I'll never find my way back," he thought and got really <u>scared</u>.

5. He stopped and <u>called</u> for help.

6. Suddenly, the mist disappeared and John was <u>annoyed</u> because he had been in such a panic.

**II  Find the opposites.** (8 pts.)

| weak | _____ | peaceful | _____ |
| beautiful | _____ | heavy | _____ |
| famous | _____ | poor | _____ |
| serious | _____ | interesting | _____ |

**III  Verbs with prepositions** (14 pts.)

Put in the correct prepositions to complete the sentences.

PAUL: I don't know this word. I must find _____ what it means.
SARA: Why don't you look it _____? By the way, I'm looking _____ my watch. Have you seen it?

PAUL: No, I haven't.

MRS RYAN: I'm going _____ now. Can you two look _____ your little sisters while I'm away? It won't be long until your father comes home.

SARA: Of course. Maybe I could get a new watch for my birthday? Oh, I'm looking _____ _____ my party. I'll put my new dress _____ and I'll get lots of presents.

MRS RYAN: Come on, Sara, you'll find your watch, I'm sure of that. I only wish your father was already here. If he got _____ earlier, he wouldn't be that late in the evenings. Paul, can you please turn the TV _____? It's too loud.

PAUL: But Mum, there's a report about the plane that crashed while taking _____. I'm interested _____ that!

MR RYAN: Hello everyone! Sorry, I'm late. My car broke _____ on the way home. I had to take the bus. Maybe I should buy a motor bike. Then I would be home sooner.

MRS RYAN: You will never grow _____, Mike. Could you please take care of Emma and Amber while I'm at the supermarket?

**Solution**

I **Find a synonym for each word underlined.**

*Hinweis: Für das Verfassen von englischen Texten ist es sehr nützlich, einen großen und abwechslungsreichen Wortschatz zu haben. Wenn Du ein Wort nicht ersetzen kannst oder dir kein Gegenstück dazu einfällt, konzentriere dich zunächst auf die anderen Aufgaben und versuche es später noch einmal. Oft können dir einsprachige Wörterbücher bei der Suche helfen.*

1. John could not see the tree anymore because of the **fog**.
2. Finally, it became **obvious** to him that he had lost his way.
3. John was **crazy** with anger.
4. "I'll never find my way back," he thought and got really **frightened**.
5. He stopped and **cried/shouted** for help.
6. Suddenly, the mist disappeared and John was **angry** because he had been in such a panic.

II **Find the opposites.**

| | | | | |
|---|---|---|---|---|
| weak | – **strong/powerful/tough** | | peaceful | – **loud/violent** |
| beautiful | – **ugly** | | heavy | – **light** |
| famous | – **unknown** | | poor | – **wealthy/rich** |
| serious | – **funny/silly** | | interesting | – **boring** |

III **Verbs with prepositions**

*Hinweis: Viele englische Verben werden mit bestimmten Adverben oder Präpositionen verbunden und erhalten dadurch eine neue Bedeutung. Achte deshalb auf die richtige Kombination von Adverb bzw. Präposition und Verb.*
*Beispiel: „to look at sth." (etwas anschauen), „to blow sth. up" (etwas aufblasen/sprengen)*

PAUL: I don't know this word. I must find **out** what it means.

SARA: Why don't you look it **up**? By the way, I'm looking **for** my watch. Have you seen it?

PAUL: No, I haven't.

MRS RYAN: I'm going **out** now. Can you two look **after** your little sisters while I'm away? It won't be long until your father comes home.

SARA: Of course. Maybe I could get a new watch for my birthday? Oh, I'm looking **forward to** my party. I'll put my new dress **on** and I'll get lots of presents.

MRS RYAN: Come on, Sara, you'll find your watch, I'm sure of that. I only wish your father was already here. If he got **up** earlier, he wouldn't be that late in the evenings. Paul, can you please turn the TV **down**? It's too loud.

PAUL: But Mum, there's a report about the plane that crashed while taking **off**. I'm interested **in** that!

MR RYAN: Hello everyone! Sorry, I'm late. My car broke **down** on the way home. I had to take the bus. Maybe I should buy a motor bike. Then I would be home sooner.

MRS RYAN: You will never grow **up**, Mike. Could you please take care of Emma and Amber while I'm at the supermarket?

**Notenschlüssel:**

| 1 | 2 | 3 | 4 | 5 | 6 |
|---|---|---|---|---|---|
| 28–26 | 25–22 | 21–18 | 17–14 | 13–9 | 8–0 |

## Test 6
### Schwerpunkte: *The passive, vocabulary*

**20 minutes**

**I  The passive: Sydney – Gateway to Australia** (10 pts.)
Mark the correct form to be used in the sentence.

Sydney, the capital of New South Wales, _____ (1) by millions of tourists every year. The city offers a rich variety of things to see and do. Most points of interest can _____ (2) on foot or by public transport.

Start your tour in Sydney Cove. On a harbour tour you _____ (3) the city's most famous sights: the Harbour Bridge and the Opera House. The Harbour Bridge with its massive 503 metres is nicknamed "the coathanger". After the bridge _____ (4) for more than 100 years, it _____ (5) in 1932. Pier One, an old shipping terminal near the bridge, _____ (6) as an entertainment area with seafood restaurants, taverns, shops and markets.

The Opera House at Bennelong Park is Sydney's most spectacular landmark. While it _____ (7) in the 1960s, there were heated discussions about technical problems and rising costs. But since its completion in 1973 crowds of visitors from all over the world _____ (8) by its ship-like architecture and high quality performances.

Sydney is also a paradise for shoppers and food lovers. Australian gifts and souvenirs can _____ (9) in "The Rocks" area, seafood and exotic dishes _____ (10) by restaurants around the harbour, in Chinatown and other parts of the city.

| | | | | | |
|---|---|---|---|---|---|
| **1** | ☐ has been visited | ☐ | is visited | ☐ | visited |
| **2** | ☐ be reaching | ☐ | reach | ☐ | be reached |
| **3** | ☐ will be shown | ☐ | are being shown | ☐ | would be shown |
| **4** | ☐ has been planned | ☐ | had been planned | ☐ | was being planned |

| | | | | | |
|---|---|---|---|---|---|
| 5 ☐ | was completed and opened | ☐ | is completed and opened | ☐ | is complete and open |
| 6 ☐ | has recently redeveloped | ☐ | has recently been redeveloped | ☐ | has been recently being redeveloped |
| 7 ☐ | has been built | ☐ | was being built | ☐ | was built |
| 8 ☐ | have been attracted | ☐ | had been attracted | ☐ | were attracted |
| 9 ☐ | buy | ☐ | bought | ☐ | be bought |
| 10 ☐ | are being offered | ☐ | are offered | ☐ | offered |

## II  Vocabulary grid: Australia (10 pts.)

Fill in the words across (1–9) to find the solution (10).

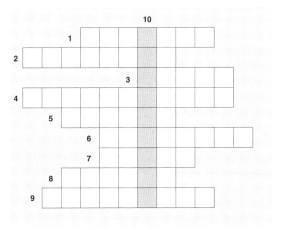

1  wild, empty country in the centre of Australia
2  big Australian animal that carries its babies in a bag-like pouch
3  this house is Sydney's most spectacular landmark
4  the guitar, the piano and the didgeridoo belong to this group
5  biggest city in Australia
6  food grilled outside
7  Australian animal that lives in trees most of the time
8  country that is not independent
9  the native people of Australia
10 Australian sports equipment that was used for hunting in the past

## III Definitions: Information about Australia (10 pts.)

Read the short text and explain the words underlined in one sentence each.

The new continent (**1**) was discovered by a Dutch sailor in 1606, but it took more than 160 years until the first English ships landed on the east coast of Australia. Many of the people on board were convicts (**2**). The early settlers (**3**) had a hard time in the strange land and climate, but with the development of the wool industry and the discovery of gold the situation improved. Today, huge sheep and cattle stations (**4**) still play an important role, but most inhabitants (**5**) of Australia live and work in the urban areas along the coast.

1 _____
2 _____
3 _____
4 _____
5 _____

**Solution**

## I The passive: Sydney – Gateway to Australia

*Hinweis:* Hier musst du die Verben ins Passiv setzen. Erklärungen und Beispiele zur Bildung des Passivs findest du in der Kurzgrammatik (S. 21/22), falls du dich bei der einen oder anderen Form noch vergewissern möchtest. Überlege für jeden einzelnen Satz, welche Zeitform du verwenden musst. Oft kannst du dies an Signalwörtern (z. B. „recently": present perfect) erkennen oder an der Zeit im vorhergehenden bzw. folgenden Satz. Hier erhältst du 1 Punkt für jede richtige Verbform.

| | | | | | |
|---|---|---|---|---|---|
| 1 | ☐ has been visited | ☑ | is visited | ☐ | visited |
| 2 | ☐ be reaching | ☐ | reach | ☑ | be reached |
| 3 | ☑ will be shown | ☐ | are being shown | ☐ | would be shown |
| 4 | ☐ has been planned | ☑ | had been planned | ☐ | was being planned |
| 5 | ☑ was completed and opened | ☐ | is completed and opened | ☐ | is complete and open |
| 6 | ☐ has recently redeveloped | ☑ | has recently been redeveloped | ☐ | has been recently being redeveloped |
| 7 | ☐ has been built | ☑ | was being built | ☐ | was built |
| 8 | ☑ have been attracted | ☐ | had been attracted | ☐ | were attracted |
| 9 | ☐ buy | ☐ | bought | ☑ | be bought |
| 10 | ☐ are being offered | ☑ | are offered | ☐ | offered |

## II Vocabulary grid: Australia

|   |   |   |   | 10 |   |   |   |   |
|---|---|---|---|---|---|---|---|---|
| 1 | O | U | T | B | A | C | K |   |
| 2 K | A | N | G | A | R | O | O |   |
|   |   |   | 3 | O | P | E | R | A |
| 4 I | N | S | T | R | U | M | E | N | T | S |
|   | 5 S | Y | D | N | E | Y |   |   |
|   |   | 6 B | A | R | B | E | C | U | E |
|   |   | 7 K | O | A | L | A |   |   |
|   | 8 C | O | L | O | N | Y |   |   |
| 9 A | B | O | R | I | G | I | N | E |

## III Definitions: Information about Australia

*Hinweis:* Die Definitionen kannst du allein mit deinem Hintergrundwissen beantworten. Versuche deine Erklärungen möglichst einfach auszudrücken. Je mehr Nebensätze du benötigst, desto komplizierter wird es für den Leser, deine Aussage noch zu verstehen. Für jede richtige Definition erhältst du 2 Punkte.

1 A continent is one of the five huge areas of land on the earth.
2 A convict is somebody who is sent to prison for a crime.
3 A settler is a person who goes to a (new) country to live there.
4 A cattle station is an Australian farm where cows and bulls are kept.
5 An inhabitant is someone who lives in a place.

## Notenschlüssel:

| 1 | 2 | 3 | 4 | 5 | 6 |
|---|---|---|---|---|---|
| 30–27 | 26–23 | 22–19 | 18–15 | 14–10 | 9–0 |

# Test 7
## Schwerpunkt: *Listening comprehension*

**15 minutes**

**Listening comprehension: A conversation at the tennis club** (Track 1)

Ben and Abby are neighbours and quite good friends. It's after the summer holidays and they are telling each other what they have been doing in the last few weeks.
Listen to the text and do the tasks.

**I  True or false? If false, correct the wrong part.** (12 pts.)

        true   false

1. Ben has been on holiday to Tenerife. ☐ ☐

2. He stayed at a camp site. ☐ ☐

3. Ben enjoyed his holiday. ☐ ☐

4. Ben looks very pale. ☐ ☐

5. Abby spent a lot of time inside. ☐ ☐

6. Ben thinks Abby's holiday was great. ☐ ☐

7. Ben wants to join Abby in Scotland next year. ☐ ☐

**II  Choose the correct answer.** (4 pts.)

Watch out: More than one answer may be right.

1. Ben could choose from a lot of sports in his holidays, namely …
    - [ ] sailing.
    - [ ] volleyball.
    - [ ] tennis.
    - [ ] badminton.

2. Abby did not enjoy her holiday because …
    - [ ] she was made fun of by other children.
    - [ ] the food tasted bad.
    - [ ] she missed her boyfriend.
    - [ ] the weather was awful.

# Solution

## Listening comprehension: A conversation at the tennis club (Transcript)

*Hinweis: Bei einem Hörtext ist es wichtig, zuerst einen Überblick über den Inhalt zu gewinnen. Lies die Einleitung und die Aufgaben genau durch, bevor du den Text anhörst. Konzentriere dich beim ersten Hören auf die erste Aufgabe. Nach dem zweiten Hören kannst du dann sicher die Multiple Choice-Aufgabe beantworten und ggf. noch Teile der ersten Aufgabe ergänzen. Halte dich nicht zu lange mit einer Lösung auf, sondern arbeite zügig und lasse einzelne Lücken frei, wenn du momentan nicht auf die richtige Antwort kommst.*

ABBY: Hi, Ben, I haven't seen you for ages. Have you been away?

BEN: Yes, we've been to Spain for a holiday.

ABBY: That sounds great. Where did you go?

BEN: We stayed in a club on the island of Mallorca. It was really fantastic.

ABBY: Did you have a chance to play tennis there?

BEN: Yes, of course. They had five tennis courts and there were lots of other sports activities, too, like sailing and windsurfing. There was even a golf course for beginners.

ABBY: I bet you had a good time. You look really healthy. I suppose you had sunny weather all the time.

BEN: That's right, it was really hot. But how about you, Abby? How was your holiday?

ABBY: Well, it was different. My parents persuaded me to go to a scout camp in Scotland for a week.

BEN: Wasn't it fun?

ABBY: You're joking! We had to sleep in uncomfortable, small tents, the food was terrible and the weather wasn't too good, either.

BEN: Really? That sounds awful. What did you do there?

ABBY: We went on some trips to old castles and museums, and one afternoon they took us to see Loch Ness. But because the weather was so bad, we spent a lot of time indoors, where we could play table tennis and darts.

BEN: That was OK, wasn't it?

ABBY: Well, it could have been worse. But then I got a bad cold and had to leave two days earlier.

BEN: What a pity. So you're happy to be home again then? You should try another kind of holiday. Why don't you come to Spain with us next year?

**I  True or false? If false, correct the wrong part.**

|   |   | true | false |
|---|---|---|---|
| 1. | Ben has been on holiday to Tenerife.<br>**Ben has been on holiday to Mallorca (Spain).** | ☐ | ✓ |
| 2. | He stayed at a camp site.<br>**He stayed at a club (on Mallorca).** | ☐ | ✓ |
| 3. | Ben enjoyed his holiday. | ✓ | ☐ |
| 4. | Ben looks very pale.<br>**He looks very healthy.** | ☐ | ✓ |
| 5. | Abby spent a lot of time inside. | ✓ | ☐ |
| 6. | Ben thinks Abby's holiday was great.<br>**Ben thinks Abby's holiday was awful/terrible.** | ☐ | ✓ |
| 7. | Ben wants to join Abby in Scotland next year.<br>**Ben wants Abby to come with him to Spain next year.** | ☐ | ✓ |

**II  Choose the correct answer.**

1. Ben could choose from a lot of sports in his holidays, namely …
   - ✓ sailing.
   - ☐ volleyball.
   - ✓ tennis.
   - ☐ badminton.

2. Abby did not enjoy her holiday because …
   - ☐ she was made fun of by other children.
   - ✓ the food tasted bad.
   - ☐ she missed her boyfriend.
   - ✓ the weather was awful.

**Notenschlüssel:**

| 1 | 2 | 3 | 4 | 5 | 6 |
|---|---|---|---|---|---|
| 16–15 | 14–13 | 12–11 | 10–8 | 7–6 | 5–0 |

# Test 8
## Schwerpunkte: *Reported speech, vocabulary*

**20 minutes**

**I   Reported speech: Talking about pop stars**   (15 pts.)

It is Tuesday morning. During break Ava and her friends are talking about their favourite pop music.

AVA: I'm going to download the new Pink album this afternoon.

LILY: I downloaded it yesterday. It's fantastic.

CHLOE: I don't like Pink so much. I'm a fan of Rihanna. Have you ever seen her on stage? I'm saving money for a ticket to her show in March.

LILY: I'd like to see Katie Perry in concert. What do you think about her funny dresses?

AVA: I can't understand why people admire her so much ….

MR BROWN: Good morning! Stop talking and go to your seats, please.

Two days later Ava is telling her sister Sophie about the conversation with her classmates:
Write down what she says and use reported speech.
Find suitable verbs to begin the sentences with (say, tell, ask …) and pay attention to what needs to be changed in indirect speech.

AVA: _____

_____

_____

_____

_____

_____

_____

Then Mr Brown came in and _____

_____

_____

## II Odd one out: Music (10 pts.)

Find the odd word out and explain your decision in one sentence each.

1. DVD – record – CD – hit
2. microphone – loudspeaker – audience – mixing desk
3. singer – guitarist – drummer – pianist
4. pop – hip-hop – opera – rock
5. chorus – choir – verse – solo

## Solution

### I Reported speech: Talking about pop stars

*Hinweis: Wiederhole noch einmal die Regeln für die indirekte Rede (S. 27/ 28), bevor du die Aufgabe bearbeitest. Achte darauf, dass du die passenden einleitenden Verben verwendest. In den meisten Sätzen solltest du besonders Pronomen und Verbformen, manchmal auch Zeitangaben verändern. Für jedes richtige einleitende Verb erhältst du einen halben Punkt, für jeden Satz, in dem alle Angleichungen an die indirekte Rede stimmen, 1 Punkt.*

AVA: I **told** Lily and Chloe that **I was going to download** the new Pink album **that** afternoon. Lily **replied** that **she had downloaded** it **the day before**. Chloe **told** us that **she didn't like** Pink so much. She **said** that **she was** a fan of Rihanna. She **asked** us **if we had ever seen** her on stage. She **told** us **she was** saving money for a ticket to her/Rihanna's show in March. Lily **answered** that **she'd/she would like** to see Katie Perry in concert. She **asked** us what **we thought** about her funny dresses. I **answered** that I **could not/ couldn't understand** why people **admired** her so much. Then Mr Brown came in and **told us to** stop talking and go to **our** seats.

### II Odd one out: Music

*Hinweis: Bei „Odd one out" musst du deine Entscheidung für das Wort, das nicht in die Reihe passt, erklären. Für jede richtige Erklärung erhältst du 2 Punkte.*

1. **hit** – A hit is a very successful song. All the other words mean a collection of songs or other kinds of data/media/carriers.
2. **audience** – An audience is a group of people who listen to music. The other words describe pieces of equipment.
3. **singer** – A singer uses his/her voice, while the other people play an instrument.
4. **opera** – Pop, rock and hip-hop are modern styles of music. An opera is a mixture between a musical performance and a play.
5. **choir** – A choir is a group of people who sing together. The other words describe parts of a song.

### Notenschlüssel:

| 1 | 2 | 3 | 4 | 5 | 6 |
|---|---|---|---|---|---|
| 25–22 | 21–18 | 17–15 | 14–12 | 11–8 | 7–0 |

**Test 9**
**Schwerpunkt:** *Listening comprehension*

**20 minutes**

**Listening comprehension: Moving to Toronto** (Track 2)

Emily's father has found a new job in Canada, so the family is moving from London to Toronto. The 14-year-old teenager will have to go to a new school and make new friends. On the plane to Canada she is talking to two Canadian students and asks them about life in Toronto.
Listen to the text and then do the tasks.

**I   Mark the correct sentences.** (10 pts.)

1. Toronto is Canada's most important city.
2. Toronto is a wonderful city for teenagers.
3. Courses in Canadian schools are all quite basic.
4. Baseball is the most popular sport in Canada.
5. Carter knows a lot about sports.
6. Emily is very interested as she is crazy about sports.
7. Pupils at state schools do not have to wear uniforms.
8. Canadians are not as keen on fashion as Europeans.
9. Hailey is interested in subcultures like goth and punk.
10. Emily would like to see Hailey and Carter again.

**II   Table completion** (10 pts.)

Use the information Emily gets and fill in the grid.

| Free-time activities in Toronto |
|---|
| • |
| • |
| • |
| **Extracurricular activities at Canadian schools** |
| • |
| • |

# Solution

## Listening comprehension: Moving to Toronto (Transcript)

*Hinweis:* Lies die Einleitung und die beiden Aufgaben genau durch, bevor du den Text anhörst! Versuche beim ersten Hören, die ganze erste Aufgabe zu bearbeiten. Dann kannst du beim zweiten Hören die zweite Aufgabe in Angriff nehmen.

EMILY: You must know I'm a bit worried about our moving to Canada. It's so far away and I don't know much about it. I wonder what life in Toronto will be like.

HAILEY: It's a great place for young people and even though it's not Canada's largest city, it's divided into many neighbourhoods with lots of trendy shops and restaurants. And you'll love the fantastic shopping malls, department stores and markets you can find everywhere.

CARTER: Girls are only interested in shopping! There's loads of other stuff to do. They have international music festivals and concerts in Toronto, and there are amusement parks like "Canada's Wonderland".

EMILY: That doesn't sound too bad. I hope I'll have enough time to explore the city, what with school and all that …

HAILEY: Well, schools in Canada aren't too difficult. You can choose between general and advanced studies. Advanced courses will lead to university – but you'll have to work quite hard …

CARTER: Don't worry; school can be fun, too. Like in the US, there are lots of after-school activities, mainly sports like basketball, football, soccer and hockey. Ice hockey is our national sport. There's even a Hockey Hall of Fame in Toronto – don't miss it!

EMILY: Actually I'm not too keen on sports, but I like music and dancing. I hope I won't have problems fitting in and finding new friends.

HAILEY: I'm sure you'll be all right. Every school offers music, dance and drama clubs you can join. I bet you'll make lots of new friends soon.

EMILY: Do they have school uniforms in Canada? How do teens dress?

CARTER: Only private schools in Canada have school uniforms. Most of us dress the same way the young people in the US do – jeans and T-shirts. Canada is a very casual place, not as fashion-conscious as Europe.

HAILEY: But *I'm* really interested in fashion. Many Canadian girls like trendy styles. And in the cities you can see people who dress for a particular subculture, like goths, punks or hip-hoppers.

EMILY: Oh, look, I think we're almost there. I'd better go back to my seat now. Well, thanks for all the information. I hope I'll be able to see you again when we've settled into our new home. Let's exchange phone numbers as soon as we're allowed to switch our phones on again.

CARTER: Right. See you later, then.

HAILEY: See you.

## I  Mark the correct sentences.

1. Toronto is Canada's most important city. ☐
2. Toronto is a wonderful city for teenagers. ✓
3. Courses in Canadian schools are all quite basic. ☐
4. Baseball is the most popular sport in Canada. ☐
5. Carter knows a lot about sports. ✓
6. Emily is very interested as she is crazy about sports. ☐
7. Pupils at state schools do not have to wear uniforms. ✓
8. Canadians are not as keen on fashion as Europeans. ✓
9. Hailey is interested in subcultures like goth and punk. ☐
10. Emily would like to see Hailey and Carter again. ✓

## II  Table completion

| Free-time activities in Toronto |
|---|
| • *you can go shopping in the malls, department stores and at markets* <br> • *there are international music festivals and concerts* <br> • *there are amusement parks like "Canada's Wonderland"* |
| **Extracurricular activities at Canadian schools** |
| • *sports (e.g. baseball, football, soccer, hockey)* <br> • *music, dance and drama clubs* |

## Notenschlüssel:

| 1 | 2 | 3 | 4 | 5 | 6 |
|---|---|---|---|---|---|
| 20–19 | 18–16 | 15–13 | 12–10 | 9–7 | 6–0 |

**Test 10**
**Schwerpunkt:** *If-clauses (type I–III)*

**20 minutes**

**I  If-clauses: Teenagers and their problems** (10 pts.)

Put in the correct forms of the verbs.

MIA: If I _____ *(not/have)* to do my Maths homework, I could spend more time with my friends.

ISLA: I always get presents from my parents if I _____ *(do)* really well. That's why I work so much. They _____ _____ *(not/buy)* me a new BMX bike if I had failed the exam. I'm sure if you _____ _____ *(work)* harder, you would pass next week's Maths test easily.

MIA: But homework is so boring! If someone _____ *(write)* my essays for me, I would pay him a lot. Anyway, I can't work this evening – I need to phone Josh. He won't go out with me if I _____ *(not/call)* him tonight.

ISLA: Well, at least there's an easy solution to your problems. It's different with Linus. He would be happy if he _____ _____ *(not/laugh)* at by our classmates.

MIA: I guess you're right. Just think about Mary. If she _____ *(move)* to Chicago, she will lose her old friends.

ISLA: Oh no, the bell is ringing. Hurry up, Mia. If we're late again, we _____ *(punish)* by Mr Smith.

MIA: That was just bad luck. We wouldn't have been told off last time if Mr Smith _____ *(be)* late as usual. Nobody expected him to be on time!

**II  Complete the sentences using your own ideas.** (10 pts.)

1. If I hadn't missed the bus, _____

2. If you watch TV all the time, _____

3. If I had more money, _____

4. If I can't go to the party, _____

5. If we had a pet, _____

**Solution**

**I  If-clauses: Teenagers and their problems**

*Hinweis: Wenn du dich wegen der Zeitenfolge im if-Satz unsicher fühlst, solltest du noch einmal die Regeln zur Bildung der Bedingungssätze im Englischen auf Seite 23 und 24 wiederholen. Entscheidend ist im Grunde genommen immer die vorausgehende Zeit im if-Satz oder Hauptsatz bzw. die Wahrscheinlichkeit, mit der das erwähnte Ereignis (noch) eintreten kann.*

MIA: If I **didn't have** to do my Maths homework, I could spend more time with my friends.

ISLA: I always get presents from my parents if I **do** really well. That's why I work so much. They **wouldn't have bought** me a new BMX bike if I had failed the exam. I'm sure if you **worked** harder, you would pass next week's Maths test easily.

MIA: But homework is so boring! If someone **wrote** my essays for me, I would pay him a lot. Anyway, I can't work this evening – I need to phone Josh. He won't go out with me if I **don't call** him tonight.

ISLA: Well, at least there's an easy solution to your problems. It's different with Linus. He would be happy if he **wasn't laughed** at by our classmates.

MIA: I guess you're right. Just think about Mary. If she **moves** to Chicago, she will lose her old friends.

ISLA: Oh no, the bell is ringing. Hurry up, Mia. If we're late again, we **will/'ll be punished** by Mr Smith.

MIA: That was just bad luck. We wouldn't have been told off last time if Mr Smith **had been** late as usual. Nobody expected him to be on time!

**II  Complete the sentences using your own ideas.**

*Hinweis: Hier kannst du dir selbst passende Folgen für die if-Sätze ausdenken. Wichtig ist dabei wieder, auf die richtige Zeitform zu achten.*

1. If I hadn't missed the bus, **I wouldn't have been late for school.**
2. If you watch TV all the time, **you won't be able to meet your friends.**
3. If I had more money, **I would buy some nice clothes.**
4. If I can't go to the party, **I will be very sad.**
5. If we had a pet, **we would have to look after it.**

**Notenschlüssel:**

| 1 | 2 | 3 | 4 | 5 | 6 |
|---|---|---|---|---|---|
| 20–19 | 18–16 | 15–13 | 12–10 | 9–7 | 6–0 |

# Test 11
## Schwerpunkt: *Analysing a cartoon*

**15 minutes**

**Analysing a cartoon**

Look at the cartoon and complete the following tasks.

1. Describe what you can see in the cartoon. (6 pts.)

2. Explain what is funny about the cartoon. What do you think the cartoonist wants to say? (6 pts.)

3. How do you feel about computer games? Write about 100 words. (15 pts.)

## Solution

### Analysing a cartoon

*Hinweis:* Cartoons verbinden Bild und Text, um Personen oder Verhaltensweisen zu kritisieren und sich über ein (meist aktuelles) Problem lustig zu machen. Bei der Analyse eines Cartoons solltest du zunächst das Bild genau beschreiben und es dann mit dem Text in Zusammenhang bringen. Nützliche Redewendungen bei der Bildbeschreibung sind: „in the (centre of the) picture", „in the foreground/in the background", „next to/in front of/behind", „on the left/right".
Oft besteht ein Widerspruch zwischen dem Cartoon und einer Aussage, die eine der gezeichneten Personen macht. Hier ist meistens die Botschaft zu finden, die der Zeichner dem Betrachter vermitteln will. Bei den ersten beiden Arbeitsaufträgen bekommst du maximal 4 Punkte auf den Inhalt und 2 Punkte auf die Sprache, bei der Bewertung der dritten Aufgabe werden maximal 5 Punkte auf den Inhalt und 10 Punkte auf die Sprache verteilt.

1. The cartoon shows a boy sitting in an armchair in his family's living room, reading a Harry Potter novel. His mother is standing next to him. She is wearing a dress and comfortable shoes and is pointing at the TV and a playstation in the background. She is obviously angry because her son is reading a book instead of playing with his expensive new playstation.

2. The cartoon is funny because the mother in the picture is criticising her son for reading a book. Normally children prefer to watch TV or play on their computer and parents worry about that. I think the cartoonist wants to point out that there are books that are more interesting than computer games. Maybe the cartoonist also wants to show that parents today have accepted that their children play computer games. This is why they buy them all the expensive equipment even if the children only want it because their friends own the same things.

3. I like playing computer games in my spare time, but I have many other hobbies, too. I have my own Nintendo DS with many games like Mario Kart and Pokemon. Some time ago my parents bought a Wii, so we can play games on the big TV screen, but we also do sports or play party games together. I think computer games can be very interesting and exciting. Most young people today have their own portable consoles and play games when they have the time to do so. You can connect with your friends or exchange games, so computers do not make you lonely.

### Notenschlüssel:

| 1 | 2 | 3 | 4 | 5 | 6 |
|---|---|---|---|---|---|
| 27–25 | 24–22 | 21–18 | 17–14 | 13–9 | 8–0 |

# Test 12
**Schwerpunkt:** *Mind map*

**10 minutes**

## Mind map: Films (29 pts.)

Fill in the mind map collecting words connected with the word field "film".
Find as many words as possible for each group.

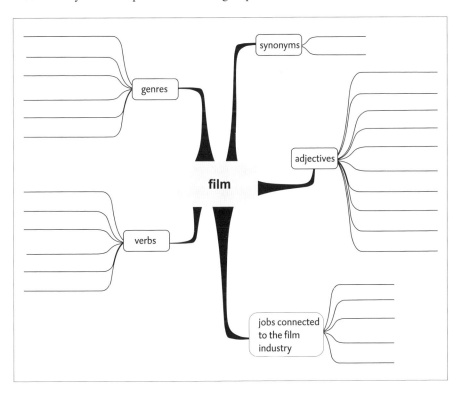

# Solution

## Mind map: Films

*Hinweis: In einer Mindmap sammelt man Begriffe, die man mit einem Thema verbindet. So kann man den englischen Wortschatz auf kreative Weise wiederholen. In Zukunft fällt es dir so sicher leichter, zum Thema „Film" etwas zu schreiben oder zu erzählen, da du dich besser an verschiedene Ausdrücke erinnerst. Schreibe zunächst alle deine Ideen entsprechend den vorgegebenen Kategorien auf. Achte dabei auch auf die richtige Wortart (Adjektiv, Verb, Nomen). Der Lösungsvorschlag kann natürlich nur einen Teil der möglichen Vokabeln enthalten. Für jedes richtige Wort erhältst du 1 Punkt.*

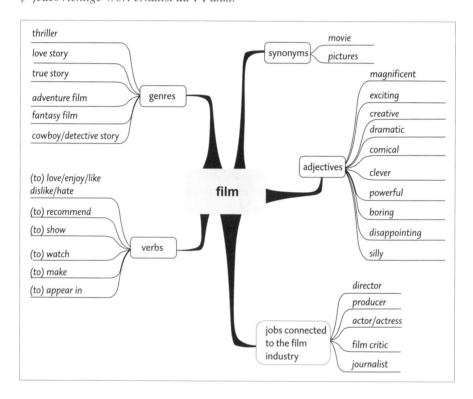

## Notenschlüssel:

| 1 | 2 | 3 | 4 | 5 | 6 |
|---|---|---|---|---|---|
| 29–27 | 26–23 | 22–19 | 18–15 | 14–10 | 9–0 |

# Test 13
**Schwerpunkte:** *Mediation, comment*

**20 minutes**

**I   Mediation: The Metropolitan Tower** (12 pts.)

You have found this advertisement for apartments in a New York tower block in an American magazine.
Your mother has also seen it and wants to know what it is about.
Complete the dialogue.

### LIVING IN THE METROPOLITAN TOWER

**Have you ever thought of living right in the heart of Manhattan? Close to Central Park and the Hudson River?**

Attending the Broadway theaters, shopping in the finest stores on Madison Avenue, going for a jog in the park, or simply walking to work on Sixth or Seventh Avenue: This is all easily done when your address is 146 West 57th Street. The Metropolitan Tower is a 78-story luxury skyscraper with sensational New York City views in all directions. Innovative in both engineering and design, the triangular glass-covered building rises to a height of 716 feet, housing 235 apartment units. The Metropolitan Tower also provides private dining at Club Metropolitan and a health club with swimming pool and excellent service.

We offer 2 – 4-room apartments for rent, starting from $3,900.

All units are equipped with individual heat and air conditioning systems and a 24-hour security service.

For further information contact:
Manhattan Management Co., Inc.
504 West 70th Street
New York, NY 10074
Tel (212) 488 5600
contact@mmco.com

MUTTER: Der Wolkenkratzer sieht ja futuristisch aus. Worum geht es denn in der Anzeige?

DU: _____

_____

MUTTER: Aha. Wo liegt der Metropolitan Tower genau?

DU: _____

_____

MUTTER: Warum sollten Leute denn mitten in Manhattan wohnen wollen?

DU: _____

_____

MUTTER: Und wie viel kosten die Wohnungen?

DU: _____

_____

MUTTER: Das ist ja eine Menge Geld. Was bekommt man denn dafür geboten?

DU: _____

_____

MUTTER: Na ja, das ist wohl mehr etwas für Manager oder Stars! Aber ich möchte nicht unbedingt in einem Hochhaus in dieser Riesenstadt leben, auch wenn ich viel Geld hätte!

## II  Comment: Living in the countryside (18 pts.)

You prefer living in the countryside to staying in a metropolis.
Give reasons for your opinion and write about 100 words.

_____

_____

_____

_____

_____

**Solution**

## I Mediation: The Metropolitan Tower

*Hinweis: Bei dieser Aufgabe musst du die nötigen Informationen aus dem Text auswählen und an der passenden Stelle in den deutschen Dialog einfügen. Oft ist es hilfreich, sich geeignete Textpassagen zu markieren, damit man sie dann schneller wiederfindet. Lies die gekennzeichneten Textstellen in jedem Fall genau durch, um zu überprüfen, ob sie tatsächlich eine Antwort auf die Frage der Mutter beinhalten und überlege dir dann die deutschen Formulierungen. Wenn dir einige englische Begriffe unbekannt vorkommen, versuche ihre Bedeutung aus dem Satzzusammenhang zu erschließen. Für jede fehlerfreie Antwort erhältst du 2 Punkte, für die letzte, besonders ausführliche Information gleich 4 Punkte.*

MUTTER: Der Wolkenkratzer sieht ja futuristisch aus. Worum geht es denn in der Anzeige?

DU: Man kann im Metropolitan Tower in New York Wohnungen mieten.

MUTTER: Aha. Wo liegt der Metropolitan Tower genau?

DU: Mitten in Manhattan, in der Nähe von Central Park und Hudson (River).

MUTTER: Warum sollten Leute denn mitten in Manhattan wohnen wollen?

DU: Man kann von dort aus alles leicht und zum Teil sogar zu Fuß erreichen: die Theater am Broadway, die schönsten Läden, den Park und den Arbeitsplatz.

MUTTER: Und wie viel kosten die Wohnungen?

DU: Hier steht, dass die Wohnungen ab 3.900 Dollar gemietet werden können.

MUTTER: Das ist ja eine Menge Geld. Was bekommt man denn dafür geboten?

DU: Es sind Luxuswohnungen mit zwei bis vier Zimmern, Klimaanlage und toller Aussicht. Im Haus gibt es ein Restaurant und einen Fitness-Club mit Schwimmbecken für die Bewohner.

MUTTER: Na ja, das ist wohl mehr etwas für Manager oder Stars! Aber ich möchte nicht unbedingt in einem Hochhaus in dieser Riesenstadt leben, auch wenn ich viel Geld hätte!

## II Comment: Living in the countryside

*Hinweis: Hier musst du eine vorgebene Meinung mit passenden Argumenten begründen. Überlege dir drei bis vier überzeugende Aspekte und beginne mit dem am wenigsten stichhaltigen. Verbinde die einzelnen Gründe durch geeignete „linker" (z. B. „then", „moreover", „finally"). Für den Inhalt des Textes erhältst du maximal 6, für die Sprache 12 Punkte.*

I would prefer to live in the countryside because life there is much more comfortable. First of all, flats in the city are quite small and very expensive while houses in the countryside are much bigger. Then, in the centre of the city there are a lot of problems like traffic, noise, pollution and violence. In the countryside the air is clean and everything is quieter. It is also easier to get to know your neighbours and find friends in a small town or a village than in a huge city. All in all, I would give up the advantages of the city for a house with a garden of my own in the country.

(115 words)

**Notenschlüssel:**

| 1 | 2 | 3 | 4 | 5 | 6 |
|---|---|---|---|---|---|
| 30–27 | 26–23 | 22–19 | 18–15 | 14–10 | 9–0 |

# Test 14
**Schwerpunkte:** *Verb forms (active/passive, use of tenses)*

**15 minutes**

**The history of the Native Americans** (20 pts.)

Fill in the correct verb forms.

When the first white men _____ (explore) America, Indian tribes _____ (live) there for thousands of years. They _____ (spread) out over the whole continent, _____ (develop) different languages and customs.
But with the arrival of an increasing number of colonists from Europe, the Indians of the Eastern regions _____ (force) to leave their homelands. In 1789 the US government _____ (promise) that no more land _____ (take) away from the Indians against their will. But this promise _____ (soon/break) by the white settlers.
Everyone _____ (hear) about the terrible wars that _____ (fight) between the Indians and the U.S. army in the 19th century and _____ (end) with the complete defeat of the Native Americans. The survivors _____ (send) to reservations, small areas of land that _____ (not/be) good for farming.
Today only 25 % of the Native Americans _____ (still/live) on land that belongs to their tribe. In recent years Indian councils _____ (give) the right to act like state governments. Tribes _____ (found) industries, tourist hotels and casinos to improve the economic situation of their members.
Nobody _____ (know) what the future _____ (bring). Still, it is a fact that the number of Americans who _____ (be) proud to be Natives _____ (rise).

**Solution**

## The history of the Native Americans

*Hinweis: Lies dir den Text genau durch und achte sowohl auf den Sinn der Sätze als auch auf die Signalwörter für die Verwendung der Zeiten. Oft lassen sich aufgrund des Kontextes die benötigten Grammatikformen gut erschließen. Wenn du dir unsicher bist, überlege dir, in welcher Zeit der Satz im Deutschen gestanden hätte. Mitunter kann dir dieser Gedanke schon weiterhelfen. Wiederhole auch die Grundregeln auf den Seiten 14 bis 22, wenn du nicht weiter weißt.*

When the first white men **explored/were exploring** America, Indian tribes **had been living/had lived** there for thousands of years. They **had spread** out over the whole continent, **developing** different languages and customs.

But with the arrival of an increasing number of colonists from Europe, the Indians of the Eastern regions **were forced** to leave their homelands. In 1789 the US government **promised** that no more land **would be taken** away from the Indians against their will. But this promise **was soon broken** by the white settlers.

Everyone **has heard** about the terrible wars that **were fought** between the Indians and the U.S. army in the 19th century and **ended** with the complete defeat of the Native Americans. The survivors **were sent** to reservations, small areas of land that **were not** good for farming.

Today only 25 % of the Native Americans **are still living/still live** on land that belongs to their tribe. In recent years Indian councils **have been given** the right to act like state governments. Tribes **have founded** industries, tourist hotels and casinos to improve the economic situation of their members.

Nobody **knows** what the future **will bring**. Still, it is a fact that the number of Americans who **are** proud to be Natives **is rising/has risen**.

**Notenschlüssel:**

| 1 | 2 | 3 | 4 | 5 | 6 |
|---|---|---|---|---|---|
| 20–19 | 18–16 | 15–13 | 12–10 | 9–7 | 6–0 |

**Test 15**
**Schwerpunkt:** *Listening comprehension*

**15 minutes**

**Listening comprehension: Spider Woman – a Navajo legend** (Track 3)

Listen to a Navajo woman telling one of her people's famous old legends and then do the tasks.

**I   Underline and correct the facts that are wrong.** (9 pts.)

1. A long time ago a group of Navajo Indians lived in a canyon in Utah.

   _____

2. They believed in powers like the Moon God and his wife Spider Woman.

   _____

3. Children were told that Spider Woman lived in a cave in the canyon.

   _____

4. One day a young Navajo was collecting wood in a far-off part of the canyon.

   _____

5. There he met an enemy and tried to kill him.

   _____

6. While the enemy was chasing him, he was looking for his friends.

   _____

7. But then he saw Spider Rock and climbed it with the help of a ladder.

   _____

8. The young man was very happy when he saw who had rescued him.

   _____

9. Later he ran home to write a book about his adventure.

   _____

## II  Comprehension: Short answers (5 pts.)

Answer the questions in one to five words.

1. What did the caves save the Navajo from? **(2 aspects)**

   _____

   _____

2. What did the Navajo traditionally eat? **(2 aspects)**

   _____

   _____

3. What did the Navajo use baskets and pots for?

   _____

   _____

# Solution

## Listening comprehension: Spider Woman – a Navajo legend (Transcript)

*Hinweis: Lies die Aufgaben aufmerksam durch, bevor du den Text zweimal anhörst! Die Wörter „ancestor" (Vorfahre), „tribesman" (Stammesangehöriger) und „silken" (aus Seide) sind dir vielleicht noch nicht bekannt. Du kannst ihre Bedeutung jedoch aus dem Zusammenhang erraten oder sie dir über ähnliche Wörter (wie z. B. „tribe" oder „tribal") selbst erschließen. Lies dir die Arbeitsaufträge genau durch, bevor du das Hörverstehen startest. Versuche wieder, dich beim ersten Hören auf die erste Aufgabe zu konzentrieren und beim zweiten Hören ausschließlich die nächste Aufgabe zu bearbeiten.*

A long time ago a group of Navajo people, our ancestors, lived in a canyon in Arizona. The canyon was very deep and surrounded by high red- and orange-coloured cliffs. Our people found caves there, high above the canyon floor, where they were safe from storms, floods and their enemies. So the Navajo lived in peace. They hunted animals, planted corn, and made beautiful baskets and pots to keep their food in.

At that time they still believed in the old gods, like the Sun God and his wife Spider Woman. Mothers used to show their children a high, pointed rock at the bottom of the canyon and tell them: "This is the place where Spider Woman lives. She has always helped our people to defeat our enemies and even today she is watching you from the top of Spider Rock. So be good and don't make her angry."

One day a young Navajo was hunting in a far-off part of the canyon. Suddenly he met an enemy tribesman, who lifted his spear and wanted to kill him. The peaceful Navajo tried to escape and ran for his life, but the other man, who was fast and strong, chased him along the canyon. When the young man noticed that he could not outrun his enemy, he looked for a place to hide. But the caves of his people were on the other side of the canyon. There was only Spider Rock, right in front of him. What could he do?

The rock was too steep to climb, but suddenly he saw a silken rope hanging from its top. The young man grabbed the rope and with its help he was pulled up the rock and escaped from his enemy, who could not follow him.

When the young man reached the top he saw a beautiful, tall woman standing in front of him. He was struck by surprise and fear because he realized that Spider Woman had rescued him. She was very friendly and told him to stay with her until his enemy had gone. Later, when everything was safe, the young man climbed down with the help of the magic rope and ran home as fast as he could to tell his people how Spider Woman had saved his life.

**I  Underline and correct the facts that are wrong.**

1. A long time ago a group of Navajo Indians lived in a canyon in <u>Utah</u>.
   **Arizona**
2. They believed in powers like the <u>Moon</u> God and his wife Spider Woman.
   **Sun**
3. Children were told that Spider Woman lived <u>in a cave</u> in the canyon.
   **on a rock**
4. One day a young Navajo was <u>collecting wood</u> in a far-off part of the canyon.
   **hunting**
5. There he met an enemy <u>and</u> tried to kill him.
   **who**
6. While the enemy was chasing him, he was looking for <u>his friends</u>.
   **a place to hide / hiding place**
7. But then he saw Spider Rock and climbed it with the help of a <u>ladder</u>.
   **(silken / magic) rope**
8. The young man was <u>very happy</u> when he saw who had rescued him.
   **surprised / afraid**
9. Later he ran home to <u>write a book</u> about his adventure.
   **tell his people**

**II  Comprehension: Short answers**

1. storms / floods / the weather, enemies
2. animals, corn
3. to keep food in

**Notenschlüssel:**

| 1 | 2 | 3 | 4 | 5 | 6 |
|---|---|---|---|---|---|
| 14–13 | 12–11 | 10–9 | 8–7 | 6–5 | 4–0 |

# Test 16
## Schwerpunkt: *Relative clauses*

**20 minutes**

**I Swansea at a glance** (11 pts.)

Read the brochure about Swansea with information about the city and its surroundings.
Complete the sentences with relative pronouns (except for "that") and commas where necessary.
Leave out the relative pronoun (and make contact clauses) if possible.

This is a short guide for tourists _____ want to explore Swansea and its surroundings in a few days. We recommend that you start your tour at the Marina Quarter, the part of the city _____ was redeveloped in the 1980s and offers visitors hotels, a waterside walkway with cafés and pubs and a shopping area.

Visit the National Waterfront Museum _____ shows exhibitions on Wales' fascinating history of industry and invention. Poetry lovers should not miss the Dylan Thomas Centre and Theatre.

The celebrated Welsh poet _____ life was closely linked with the city is one of the famous personalities _____ Swansea is proud of. West of the city you can visit the pretty seaside village of Mumbles and the Gower Peninsula with a coastline _____ attracts thousands of nature lovers every year. The area is a great favourite with hikers and bird watchers, but also surfers _____ find ideal conditions at the Atlantic beaches.

## II  Lots of questions (10 pts.)

Your exchange partner Zac from Swansea is staying with you. On the way to school he asks a lot of questions.
Give Zac an answer by using relative pronouns.
Use contact clauses where possible.

ZAC: Where is your school?
YOU: It's _____
*(old building/you can see it on the hill).* Let's hurry up or Mr Mayr will get angry.

ZAC: Who's Mr Mayr?
YOU: _____
*(teacher/you saw him at the railway station yesterday).* Ah, there's Nele.

ZAC: And who is Nele?
YOU: _____
*(girl/her mother works at the tourist information).* But where is Fynn?

ZAC: Who is Fynn?
YOU: _____
*(friend/I play with him in the "Fußball" team)*

ZAC: And what is "Fußball"?
YOU: _____
*(sport/I like it best)*

# Solution

## I  Swansea at a glance

*Hinweis:* In dieser Aufgabe soll zwischen notwendigen und nicht notwendigen Relativsätzen „defining/non-defining relative clauses" bzw. „contact clauses" unterschieden werden. Um eine Entscheidung treffen zu können, musst du dich fragen, ob der Relativsatz zum Verständnis des Textes notwendig ist oder nur zusätzliche Informationen zu einer bestimmten Person oder Sache gibt. Für die Entscheidung für bzw. gegen einen „contact clause" ist die Frage ausschlaggebend, ob das Relativpronomen weggelassen werden kann, ohne dass der Satz unverständlich wird. Wenn dir die Lösung der Aufgabe schwer fällt, lies noch einmal in der Kurzgrammatik auf den Seiten 25 und 26 nach. Für jedes richtig eingesetzte Relativpronomen **und** Komma erhältst du 1 Punkt.

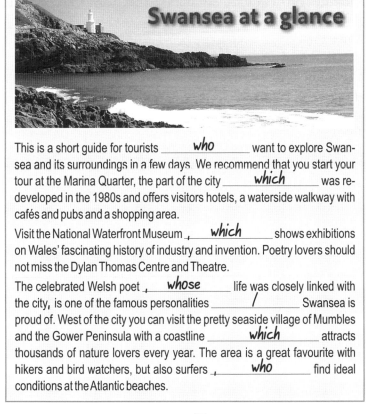

This is a short guide for tourists __who__ want to explore Swansea and its surroundings in a few days. We recommend that you start your tour at the Marina Quarter, the part of the city __which__ was redeveloped in the 1980s and offers visitors hotels, a waterside walkway with cafés and pubs and a shopping area.

Visit the National Waterfront Museum **,** __which__ shows exhibitions on Wales' fascinating history of industry and invention. Poetry lovers should not miss the Dylan Thomas Centre and Theatre.

The celebrated Welsh poet **,** __whose__ life was closely linked with the city**,** is one of the famous personalities __/__ Swansea is proud of. West of the city you can visit the pretty seaside village of Mumbles and the Gower Peninsula with a coastline __which__ attracts thousands of nature lovers every year. The area is a great favourite with hikers and bird watchers, but also surfers **,** __who__ find ideal conditions at the Atlantic beaches.

## II  Lots of questions

> *Hinweis:* Hier werden Definitionen gesucht. Verbinde dazu die vorgegebenen Informationen durch Relativpronomen, aber lasse die Pronomen aus, wenn sie nicht notwendig sind und bilde stattdessen einen sogenannten „contact clause". Wenn dir diese Aufgabe zu schwierig ist, bilde zunächst alle Sätze mit Relativpronomen und klammere dann die Pronomen ein, auf die verzichtet werden kann. Für jeden richtig gebildeten Satz erhältst du 2 Punkte.

ZAC: Where is your school?

YOU: **It's the old building (that/which) you can see on the hill.** Let's hurry up or Mr Mayr will get angry.

ZAC: Who's Mr Mayr?

YOU: **He's the teacher (that/who) you saw at the railway station yesterday.** Ah, there's Nele.

ZAC: And who is Nele?

YOU: **She's the girl whose mother works at the tourist information.** But where is Fynn?

ZAC: Who is Fynn?

YOU: **He's the friend (that/who) I play with in the "Fußball" team.**

ZAC: And what is "Fußball"?

YOU: **It's the sport I like best.**

## Notenschlüssel:

| 1 | 2 | 3 | 4 | 5 | 6 |
|---|---|---|---|---|---|
| 21–19 | 18–16 | 15–13 | 12–10 | 9–7 | 6–0 |

# Test 17
**Schwerpunkte:** *Gerund after prepositions, mixed bag*

**20 minutes**

**I  The gerund after prepositions** (14 pts.)

Read the text of the holiday brochure and fill in the gaps with the correct prepositions and the gerund forms of the following verbs:

> find – see – welcome – ~~travel~~ – take – climb – make – visit

How _**about travelling**_ to Scotland in the summer holidays? The Scottish are famous _____ their guests feel at home.

You needn't worry _____ a suitable place to stay: Scotland offers many beautiful hotels and B&Bs.

Whether you are interested _____ ancient castles or _____ a city break in Edinburgh, we have got the perfect holiday package for you. If you are keen _____ mountains, you should choose a backpacking holiday in the Highlands.

Don't forget to visit Loch Ness. You might have a chance _____ Nessie, the famous monster.

Book your holidays now.

We are looking _____ you to Scotland this summer.

**Ask your local travel agency for more information or check in online:
Great Scottish Hotels and B&Bs @ www.itsascotsworld.co.uk**

## II  Mixed bag                                            (23 pts.)

Fill in the gaps by using verbs, adjectives, adverbs, prepositions and articles.
Keep the tenses and signal words in mind.

_____ Golden Gate Bridge lies at the entrance _____ San Francisco Bay and is _____ high that ships _____ pass under it. It links San Francisco _____ the country north of the city. It is surrounded _____ open land and there is _____ fortress at the southern side of the bridge, which _____
*(obviously/to build)* to protect the bay _____ invaders. Compared _____ Los Angeles, San Francisco is quite small: it only has about 750,000 inhabitants.

San Francisco _____ *(to use)* to be one of _____ *(important)* centres of the hippie movement. From June 16 to June 18, 1967, the Monterey International Pop Festival _____ *(to attract)* 90,000 visitors who _____ *(not/to be afraid)* _____ the long journey _____ San Francisco. Although the Monterey Pop Festival is not _____ *(famous)* Woodstock, musicians like Otis Redding _____ *(to become)* well-known because people _____ *(to enjoy/to listen)* to them.

Today the city is famous for its beautiful situation _____ San Francisco Bay, the rolling hills, an interesting mix of architecture and landmarks like _____ Golden Gate Bridge, cable cars and Chinatown. Above all, the city _____ *(to characterise)* by its multicultural population, especially Hispanics and Asian Americans, who _____ *(often/to live)* in their own typical neighbourhoods with traditional shops and restaurants.

# Solution

## I  The gerund after prepositions

*Hinweis: In dieser Aufgabe sollen passende Präpositionen und Gerundformen eingesetzt werden (z. B. "I like the idea **of going** to Scotland"). Das Gerund wird häufig nach Verbindungen von Verben/Adjektiven/Nomen mit Präpositionen gebraucht. Wenn dir die Redewendungen unbekannt vorkommen, gehe die Regeln zum Gerund auf den Seiten 11 und 12 durch. Für jede richtige Präposition und Verbform erhältst du 1 Punkt.*

How **about travelling** to Scotland in the summer holidays? The Scottish are famous **for making** their guests feel at home.

You needn't worry **about finding** a suitable place to stay: Scotland offers many beautiful hotels and B&Bs.

Whether you are interested **in visiting** ancient castles or **taking** a city break in Edinburgh, we have got the perfect holiday package for you. If you are keen **on climbing** mountains, you should choose a backpacking holiday in the Highlands.

Don't forget to visit Loch Ness. You might have a chance **of seeing** Nessie, the famous monster.

Book your holidays now.

We are looking **forward to welcoming** you to Scotland this summer.

**Ask your local travel agency for more information or check in online:
Great Scottish Hotels and B&Bs @ www.itsascotsworld.co.uk**

II  Mixed bag

> *Hinweis: In dieser Übung ist vor allem dein Sprachgefühl gefragt. In die Lücken können unterschiedliche Wörter eingesetzt werden. Welche in diesem Fall am besten geeignet sind, ist abhängig vom Satzzusammenhang. Generell können Artikel, Adjektive, unterschiedliche Zeiten sowie Adverben und Präpositionen die Lücken füllen. Bei einigen Lücken sind die Wörter bereits in ihrer Grundform vorgegeben, die richtige Wortstellung bzw. Verb- oder Steigerungsform muss allerdings noch gefunden werden. Für jeden richtig ergänzten „slot" gibt es 1 Punkt.*

**The** Golden Gate Bridge lies at the entrance **of/to** San Francisco Bay and is **so** high that ships **can** pass under it. It links San Francisco **to** the country north of the city. It is surrounded **by** open land and there is **a** fortress at the southern side of the bridge, which **was obviously built** to protect the bay **from** invaders. Compared **to** Los Angeles, San Francisco is quite small: it only has about 750,000 inhabitants.

San Francisco **used** to be one of **the most important** centres of the hippie movement. From June 16 to June 18, 1967, the Monterey International Pop Festival **attracted** 90,000 visitors who **were not/had not been afraid of** the long journey **to** San Francisco. Although the Monterey Pop Festival is not **as famous as** Woodstock, musicians like Otis Redding **became** well-known because people **enjoyed listening** to them.

Today the city is famous for its beautiful situation **on** San Francisco Bay, the rolling hills, an interesting mix of architecture and landmarks like **the** Golden Gate Bridge, cable cars and Chinatown. Above all, the city **is characterised** by its multicultural population, especially Hispanics and Asian Americans, who **often live** in their own typical neighbourhoods with traditional shops and restaurants.

**Notenschlüssel:**

| 1 | 2 | 3 | 4 | 5 | 6 |
|---|---|---|---|---|---|
| 37–33 | 32–28 | 27–23 | 22–18 | 17–12 | 11–0 |

# Test 18
## Schwerpunkt: *Cloze test*

**10 minutes**

**Cloze Test: Under-age drinking in Britain** (25 pts.)

Complete the missing words. The first letter is given already.

Britain's teenagers do not like g_____ drunk, but m_____ of those who turn to the bottle do it just to s_____ off and impress their friends with their coolness.
T_____ is the result of a study by "Drinkaware", a charity o_____ that tries to teach young p_____ about the d_____ of drinking. Researchers f_____ that 68 % of the 15- to 17-year-olds feel b_____ about being drunk. But many teens think it is i_____ to show your friends how m_____ and what type of a_____ you can drink.
Statistics point to the fact that a growing n_____ of teenagers end up in h_____. Binge drinking and related health p_____ cost the British society 2.7 billion p_____ a year.
"Drinkaware" wants b_____ and girls as young as eleven to be taught about the risks of d_____:
Parents are told to be c_____ about giving alcohol to their c_____ because about 13 % of the youngsters drink at h_____ two to three t_____ a week.
"Drinkaware" b_____ that teens need to k_____ that it is possible to go out and have f_____ without drinking alcohol.

# Solution

## Cloze Test: Under-age drinking in Britain

*Hinweis: In einem Cloze Test müssen die fehlenden Wörter aus dem Zusammenhang erschlossen werden. Die bereits vorgegebenen Anfangsbuchstaben helfen dir dabei. Wenn du Schwierigkeiten hast, den Sinn des Satzes zu erschließen, hilft es dir vielleicht, den Satz ins Deutsche zu übersetzen. Für jedes richtig ergänzte Wort erhältst du 1 Punkt.*

Britain's teenagers do not like **getting** drunk, but **most** of those who turn to the bottle do it just to **show** off and impress their friends with their coolness.
**This** is the result of a study by "Drinkaware", a charity **organisation** that tries to teach young **people** about the **dangers** of drinking. Researchers **found** that 68 % of the 15- to 17-year-olds feel **bad** about being drunk. But many teens think it is **important** to show your friends how **much** and what type of **alcohol** you can drink.
Statistics point to the fact that a growing **number** of teenagers end up in **hospital**. Binge drinking and related health **problems** cost the British society 2.7 billion **pounds** a year.
"Drinkaware" wants **boys** and girls as young as eleven to be taught about the risks of **drinking**: Parents are told to be **careful** about giving alcohol to their **children** because about 13 % of the youngsters drink at **home** two to three **times** a week.
"Drinkaware" **believes** that teens need to **know** that it is possible to go out and have **fun** without drinking alcohol.

## Notenschlüssel:

| 1 | 2 | 3 | 4 | 5 | 6 |
|---|---|---|---|---|---|
| 25–22 | 21–18 | 17–15 | 14–12 | 11–8 | 7–0 |

## Test 19
**Schwerpunkte:** *Vocabulary ("false friends"/crossword puzzle)*

**20 minutes**

**I  False friends: Julia and Charlotte in Manchester** (8 pts.)

Charlotte and her friend Julia from Berlin have decided to spend a weekend in Manchester, where Charlotte's e-pal Tim works. The girls have decided to practise their English before meeting Tim, who is still at work. Unfortunately, they do not speak English very well, so they make a lot of mistakes because they use words in the wrong way. Underline and correct the "false friends".

MANON: Let's go to the tourist information and ask for a prospect of the city.

CHARLOTTE: We'll need a card to find our way.

MANON: Oh, I almost forgot! Can you lend me your handy? I must call my parents to say I'm OK.

CHARLOTTE: I've already sent my parents a text message. I hope they'll become it in time. If not they will worry about me.

MANON: Look, there is a café around the corner. They offer scones with strawberry marmalade. I'm so hungry! Maybe Tim could pick us up here?

CHARLOTTE: Well, Tim said he had to work until 5 p.m. His chief didn't allow him to take a day off.

MANON: That's really unfair! He should look for another job. At least, this is my meaning.

CHARLOTTE: You're right. If you go inside to get your scone, would you order an orange juice for me, please? I'm not hungry and I have to spare my money for shopping tomorrow.

## II  Crossword puzzle (18 pts.)

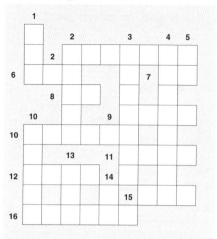

**Across:**

2  British English for "cookie"
6  This is what you need to breathe.
7  The opposite of "yes"
8  "_____ I had a lot of money, I could buy whatever I wanted."
9  "My grandparents told me they _____ very sad because their dog died."
10  A synonym for "(to) be able to buy"
11  Another word for "test"
12  Another word for "present"
15  "Don't eat it. It's my sister's. She doesn't share _____ chocolate."
16  The continent you live on

**Down:**

1  A synonym for "dinner" in the UK
2  A synonym for "short"
3  A synonym for "full of people"
4  A synonym for "(to) become/make bigger"
5  "Happy birthday _____ you!"
10  A synonym for "(to) discuss in an angry way"
13  "Please take this DVD. I bought it especially _____ you!"
14  The opposite of "down"

**Solution**

## I False friends: Manon and Charlotte in Manchester

*Hinweis:* Manche englischen Wörter klingen ähnlich wie deutsche, haben aber andere Bedeutungen (Beispiel: „mist" = Nebel). Versuche, die falschen Wörter in dem Gespräch der beiden Mädchen zu finden und ersetze sie durch die richtigen englischen Vokabeln.

MANON: Let's go to the tourist information and ask for a ~~prospect~~ of the city.     *brochure*

CHARLOTTE: We'll need a ~~card~~ to find our way.     *map*

MANON: Oh, I almost forgot! Can you lend me your ~~handy~~? I must call my parents to say I'm OK.     *mobile (phone) / cellphone*

CHARLOTTE: I've already sent my parents a text message. I hope they'll ~~become~~ it in time. If not they will worry about me.     *get*

MANON: Look, there is a café around the corner. They offer scones with strawberry ~~marmalade~~. I'm so hungry! Maybe Tim could pick us up here?     *jam*

CHARLOTTE: Well, Tim said he had to work until 5 p.m. His ~~chief~~ didn't allow him to take a day off.     *boss*

MANON: That's really unfair! He should look for another job. At least, this is my ~~meaning~~.     *opinion*

CHARLOTTE: You're right. If you go inside to get your scone, would you order an orange juice for me, please? I'm not hungry and I have to ~~spare~~ my money for shopping tomorrow.     *save*

## II  Crossword puzzle

|   | 1 T |   | 2 |   |   | 3 |   | 4 | 5 |
|---|---|---|---|---|---|---|---|---|---|
|   | E | 2 | B | I | S | C | U | I | T |
| 6 | A | I | R |   |   | R | 7 | N | O |
|   |   | 8 | I | F |   | O |   | C |   |
|   | 10 |   | E |   | 9 | W | E | R | E |
| 10 | A | F | F | O | R | D |   | E |   |
|   | R |   | 13 |   | 11 | E | X | A | M |
| 12 | G | I | F | T | 14 | D |   | S |   |
|   | U |   | O |   | U | 15 | H | E | R |
| 16 | E | U | R | O | P | E |   |   |   |

**Notenschlüssel:**

| 1 | 2 | 3 | 4 | 5 | 6 |
|---|---|---|---|---|---|
| 26–23 | 22–19 | 18–16 | 15–13 | 12–9 | 8–0 |

# Test 20
## Schwerpunkt: *Infinitive or gerund*

**10 minutes**

**Infinitive or gerund: What are you going to do on Saturday?** (26 pts.)

Molly has just returned from a holiday and is phoning her friend Erin.
Put in the correct verb forms and add prepositions if necessary.

MOLLY: Hi Erin, it's Molly.

ERIN: Molly, how are you? And how was your holiday in Austria?

MOLLY: It was great, as usual. You know _____ *(ski)* is my favourite sport.

ERIN: And the mountains in Austria are the best place _____ *(go)* if you like winter sports. Well, actually, I prefer _____ *(swim)* and _____ *(lie)* on the beach in Spain. But never mind. I'm sure you had a good time in Austria.

MOLLY: Listen, Erin, I'm going _____ *(shop)* on Saturday afternoon. Would you like _____ *(come)* with me?

ERIN: I'm sorry, I can't. My mum wants me _____ *(help)* her in the garden. I'm not too keen _____ *(paint)* the fence, but I've promised to give her a hand.

MOLLY: Then how about _____ *(go)* to the cinema in the evening?

ERIN: Well, I don't know. What's on at the weekend? The new James Bond isn't worth _____ *(watch)*, I've heard, and I don't like _____ *(waste)* my time on a silly romance if I could do something more exciting.

MOLLY: It's really difficult _____ *(find)* a good film for you. But wait ... I'm sure you will be interested _____ *(meet)* Chris and the others. Let's go to the pizza place in Chester Street.

ERIN: That's a fantastic idea. I can be at your house by 7 p.m.

MOLLY: OK then. See you on Saturday!

# Solution

**Infinitive or gerund: What are you going to do on Saturday?**

*Hinweis:* Versuche dir die Regeln zur Verwendung von Infinitiv und Gerund noch einmal ins Gedächtnis zu rufen: Welche von den beiden Formen gebraucht wird, hängt vom Verb ab. Leider musst du dir die entsprechenden Kombinationen auswendig merken, es gibt keine Eselsbrücken. Nähere Informationen findest du auf den Seiten 9 bis 12. Für jede richtige Form erhältst du 2 Punkte.

MOLLY: Hi Erin, it's Molly.

ERIN: Molly, how are you? And how was your holiday in Austria?

MOLLY: It was great, as usual. You know **skiing** is my favourite sport.

ERIN: And the mountains in Austria are the best place **to go** if you like winter sports. Well, actually, I prefer **swimming** and **lying** on the beach in Spain. But never mind. I'm sure you had a good time in Austria.

MOLLY: Listen, Erin, I'm going **shopping** on Saturday afternoon. Would you like **to come** with me?

ERIN: I'm sorry, I can't. My mum wants me **to help** her in the garden. I'm not too keen **on painting** the fence, but I've promised to give her a hand.

MOLLY: Then how about **going** to the cinema in the evening?

ERIN: Well, I don't know. What's on at the weekend? The new James Bond isn't worth **watching**, I've heard, and I don't like **to waste/wasting** my time on a silly romance if I could do something more exciting.

MOLLY: It's really difficult **to find** a good film for you. But wait ... I'm sure you will be interested **in meeting** Chris and the others. Let's go to the pizza place in Chester Street.

ERIN: That's a fantastic idea. I can be at your house by 7 p.m.

MOLLY: OK then. See you on Saturday!

**Notenschlüssel:**

| 1 | 2 | 3 | 4 | 5 | 6 |
|---|---|---|---|---|---|
| 26–23 | 22–19 | 18–16 | 15–13 | 12–9 | 8–0 |

# Test 21
## Schwerpunkt: *Picture task*

**10 minutes**

### Picture task: National Parks in the USA

The photos below show two national parks in the USA: Yosemite National Park in California and Everglades National Park in Florida.

1. Look at the pictures and describe what you can see and do in the two parks. (10 pts.)
2. Choose **one** of the parks and explain why you would like to go there. (10 pts.)

## Solution

### Picture task: National Parks in the USA

***Hinweis:** Wiederhole die für Bildbeschreibungen wichtigen Wwendungen (z. B. „in the picture", „on the (far) left/right", „in the background"). Betrachte die Bilder genau und beschreibe alle Einzelheiten, die du erkennen kannst. Im zweiten Teil der Aufgabe musst du dich für einen Park entscheiden. Überlege dir gute Argumente für deine Entscheidung, sodass du sie überzeugend vortragen kannst. Bei jeder Aufgabe erhältst du maximal 4 Punkte für den Inhalt, 6 Punkte für die Sprache.*

1. In the two pictures on the left you can see the huge rocks in Yosemite Park. They are surrounded by lots of trees and there is a river, too. The photos show that you can go rock-climbing and walking in the mountains. The pictures on the right show the Everglades National Park. You can see a car park with three cars, a small building and a long roof with a sign that offers "airboat rides" and a visit to a real Indian camp. There are three flags in front of the house. In the background, there is water and grass. The other picture shows a special speed boat in front of some palm trees so you might be able to go on a boat tour through the Everglades.

2. I would choose the Everglades National Park because I am not so keen on rock-climbing. Going on a boat tour sounds much more exciting. The wildlife in Southern Florida is also very interesting. In the Everglades National Park you can see rare birds, dolphins and even alligators. Florida has got a tropical climate and warm temperatures all year round. So you can travel there in the winter when the weather in Germany is bad.

### Notenschlüssel:

| 1 | 2 | 3 | 4 | 5 | 6 |
|---|---|---|---|---|---|
| 20–19 | 18–16 | 15–13 | 12–10 | 9–7 | 6–0 |

**Test 22**
**Schwerpunkt:** *Writing an e-mail*

**15 minutes**

**Writing an e-mail to Scotland** (18 pts.)

You and your family are planning a holiday to Scotland. Your parents are keen on exploring the Scottish countryside. You and your older brother want to visit Edinburgh. To practise your English your family has decided that you should write to the Tourist Board to find out more.

In German you have written down the questions you would like to ask:
- *Was kann man in Edinburgh unternehmen?*
- *Können wir dort einen Mietwagen buchen?*
- *Gibt es organisierte Ausflüge/Tourenvorschläge für die Highlands?*
- *Können Sie uns ein Verzeichnis mit Hotels und Pensionen in Schottland schicken?*

Write the e-mail asking for the information you need. Use a suitable introduction and ending. Write at least 100 words.

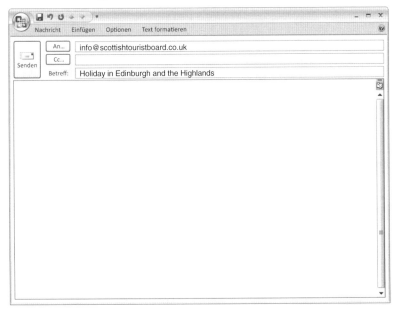

# Solution

## Writing an e-mail to Scotland

*Hinweis: Wenn du eine E-Mail an eine offizielle Stelle schreibst, musst du dieselben Regeln wie bei einem Brief einhalten. Nach der Anrede („Dear Sir or Madam") erklärst du den Grund des Schreibens und bittest um Informationen. Am Ende bedankst du dich und erklärst, dass du auf baldige Antwort wartest. Die offizielle Schlussformel lautet: „Yours faithfully ..."*
*Du erhältst 6 Punkte für den Inhalt, 12 Punkte für die Sprache.*

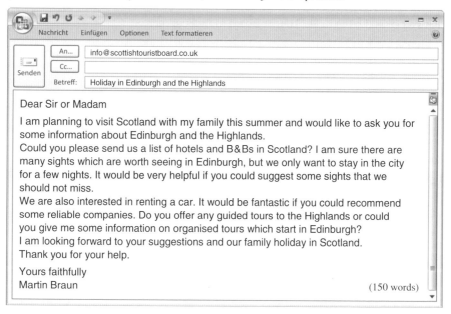

An...: info@scottishtouristboard.co.uk
Betreff: Holiday in Edinburgh and the Highlands

Dear Sir or Madam

I am planning to visit Scotland with my family this summer and would like to ask you for some information about Edinburgh and the Highlands.
Could you please send us a list of hotels and B&Bs in Scotland? I am sure there are many sights which are worth seeing in Edinburgh, but we only want to stay in the city for a few nights. It would be very helpful if you could suggest some sights that we should not miss.
We are also interested in renting a car. It would be fantastic if you could recommend some reliable companies. Do you offer any guided tours to the Highlands or could you give me some information on organised tours which start in Edinburgh?
I am looking forward to your suggestions and our family holiday in Scotland.
Thank you for your help.

Yours faithfully
Martin Braun                                                              (150 words)

## Notenschlüssel:

| 1 | 2 | 3 | 4 | 5 | 6 |
|---|---|---|---|---|---|
| 18–17 | 16–15 | 14–12 | 11–9 | 8–6 | 5–0 |

> **Test 23**
> **Schwerpunkt:** *Reading comprehension*

**20 minutes**

**Reading comprehension: Extract from *Slam***

1 I'd never met anyone quite like Alicia's mum and dad before I started going out with Alicia, and at first I thought they were dead cool – I can even remember wishing that my mum and dad were like them. Alicia's dad is like fifty or something, and he listens to hip-hop. He doesn't like it much, I don't think, but he feels
5 he should give it a chance, and he doesn't mind the language and the violence. He's got grey hair that he gets Alicia's mum to shave back – I think he has a number 2 – and he wears a stud. He teaches literature at a college, and she teaches drama, when she's not being a councillor. Or she teaches people to teach drama, something like that. She has to go into lots of different schools and talk
10 to teachers. They're all right, I suppose, Robert and Andrea, and they were really friendly at first. It's just that they think I'm stupid. They never say as much, and they try and treat me as if I'm not. But I can tell they do. I wouldn't mind, but I'm smarter than Alicia. I'm not showing off or being cocky; I just know I am. When we went to see films, she didn't understand them, and she never got
15 what anyone was laughing at in *The Simpsons*, and I had to help her with her maths. Her mum and dad helped her with her English. They still thought she was going to go to college to do something or other, and all the model stuff was just her going through a rebellious phase. As far as they were concerned, she was a genius, and I was this nice dim kid she was hanging out with. They acted as if I
20 was Ryan Briggs or someone really scummy like that, but they weren't going to officially disapprove of me because that wouldn't be cool.
At that family lunch, when I was invited because I was part of the family, I was just sitting there minding my own business when her dad asked me what I was going to do after my GCSEs.
25 'Not everybody is academic, Robert' said Alicia's mum quickly.
You see how it worked? She was trying to protect me, but what she was trying to protect me from was a question about whether I had any future at all. I mean, everyone does something after their GCSEs, don't they? Even if you sit at home watching daytime TV for the rest of your life, it's a future of sorts. But that was
30 their attitude with me – don't mention the future, because I didn't have one. And then we all had to pretend that not having a future was OK. That's what Alicia's mum should have said. 'Not everybody has a future, Robert.'

'I know not everybody is academic. I was just asking him what he wanted to do,' said Robert.
35 'He's going to do art and design at college,' said Alicia.
'Oh,' said her dad. 'Good. Excellent.'

*(507 words)*

From: Slam *by Nick Hornby, published by Penguin U.K., 2008.*

**I   Multiple matching**

Match the parts to make complete sentences.
Watch out: Two letters cannot be matched. (6 pts.)

| | | | |
|---|---|---|---|
| **1** | At first Sam likes Alicia's father because he | **a** | is not very smart and will not be really successful in later life. |
| **2** | Alicia's father listens to hip-hop music although he | **b** | wants to go to college. |
| **3** | Alicia's parents believe Sam | **c** | never tells the truth. |
| | | **d** | is interested in modelling. |
| **4** | Sam says Alicia is not very clever because she | **e** | seems to be very trendy. |
| **5** | Alicia's parents think their daughter is just having a difficult time as she | **f** | needs help at school. |
| | | **g** | does not enjoy it. |
| **6** | Alicia's father is surprised when he hears that Sam | **h** | is so friendly all the time. |

| 1 | 2 | 3 | 4 | 5 | 6 |
|---|---|---|---|---|---|
|   |   |   |   |   |   |

**II   Creative writing** (12 pts.)

Imagine you were Alicia and kept a diary. Describe the conversation between your parents and your boyfriend Sam at the family lunch (ll. 22–36).
Write a diary entry of 100 to 150 words.

## Solution

**Reading comprehension: Extract from *Slam***
### I Multiple matching

*Hinweis: Lies den Textauszug genau und achte dabei darauf, was der Erzähler Sam über sich und die anderen Personen berichtet. Die folgenden Vokabelerklärungen können dir vielleicht helfen, den Text noch besser zu verstehen: „stud" (Z. 7; Ohr- bzw. Nasenstecker), „councillor" (Z. 8; Stadträtin), „cocky" (Z. 13; großspurig), „scummy" (Z. 20; schmutzig, „wie Abschaum"). Überlege dir dann, wie die angegebenen Satzteile sinnvoll zusammengefügt werden können. Zwei der Halbsätze lassen sich nicht zuordnen. Überprüfe deshalb am Ende nochmals deine Auswahl, indem du sie mit geeigneten Textstellen vergleichst.*

| 1 | 2 | 3 | 4 | 5 | 6 |
|---|---|---|---|---|---|
| e | g | a | f | d | b |

### II Creative writing

*Hinweis: Bei dieser Aufgabe musst du dich in die Rolle von Alicia hineinversetzen. Benutze die Informationen, die du über sie erhältst und überlege dir, wie Alicia die Situation sehen könnte. Gehe auch darauf ein, was sie wohl von ihrem Freund und seinen Plänen hält. Für den Inhalt erhältst du maximal 4 Punkte, für die Sprache 8 Punkte.*

Today, Sam came over to our house to have lunch with us. Mum and Dad were very nice to him, as usual. They almost treat him like a member of the family! We were talking about school – what a boring topic. Sam didn't say much – he's always a bit shy with Mum and Dad. Then Dad asked him about what he was going to do after his GCSEs. It seemed that Sam didn't know what to say so I answered the question for him. He always talks about studying art and design at college so I really didn't understand why he didn't want to tell Dad. I answered for him because I wanted Mum and Dad to like Sam. I think Dad was totally impressed. He said "excellent" and looked a bit surprised. I'm sure Mum and Dad will soon find out that Sam is a very special person. (149 words)

### Notenschlüssel:

| 1 | 2 | 3 | 4 | 5 | 6 |
|---|---|---|---|---|---|
| 18–17 | 16–15 | 14–12 | 11–9 | 8–6 | 5–0 |

**Test 24**
**Schwerpunkt:** *Guided writing*

**20 minutes**

**Writing an article – Step by step**

**I  Preparation for text production:** (5 pts.)
   **Collecting ideas for an article**

   Your American pen friend has asked you to write a short article about soccer, the Germans' favourite sport, for his high school magazine.

   Collect ideas to explain ...
   - where soccer is played in Germany and
   - why it is so popular.

   Also think of a headline for your article.

**II  Writing the article** (15 pts.)

   Now write an article of about 150 words. Choose three arguments that you think best explain why soccer is so popular in Germany.

# Solution

## I  Preparation for text production: Collecting ideas for an article

*Hinweis:* Hier solltest du vor allem darauf eingehen, warum so viele Jugendliche Fußball spielen und warum Fußball in Deutschland allgemein so beliebt ist. Bedenke, dass ein Zeitungsartikel eine Überschrift (Schlagzeile) braucht.
Für die Überschrift erhältst du 1 Punkt, für jeden Ort einen halben Punkt und für jedes Argument 1 Punkt.

**Headline: Soccer – the Germans' favourite sport**
Places where football can be played in Germany: in backyards, at school, in clubs

Possible arguments for why football is so popular:
- it is cheap because you do not need a lot of equipment
- it is easy as the basic rules are not difficult to learn
- you never get tired of the game as there are a number of variations and tricks
- Germany has a very successful soccer team
- it is fun to watch soccer on TV as there is a great atmosphere in the stadium
- many young people dream of becoming a football star so they need to practise

## II  Writing the article

*Hinweis:* Nachdem du genügend Ideen gesammelt hast, kannst du den Artikel sicher ziemlich schnell ausformulieren. Vergiss nicht, die einzelnen Punkte logisch miteinander zu verbinden, z. B. durch Überleitungen wie „Another argument is …", „also", oder Aufzählungen wie „Firstly/Secondly/Thirdly".
Für den Inhalt erhältst du 5 Punkte und für die Sprache 10 Punkte.

**Soccer – the Germans' favourite sport**
Most boys and more and more girls are interested in soccer, and it is the kind of sport that is played almost everywhere in Germany: in backyards, at school and, above all, in many soccer clubs.
Soccer is a cheap sport: You do not need a lot of equipment – just a ball and whatever makes a nice goal. It is also quite simple. The basic rules of the game are not difficult to learn, but there are an incredible number of variations and tricks, so you will never get tired of playing soccer. But it is even more exciting to watch the "Bundesliga" (Germany's premier league). Thousands of fans who fill the huge stadiums and cheer for their favourite players create an atmosphere that is very exciting – you have to experience it yourself.         (133 words)

## Notenschlüssel:

| 1 | 2 | 3 | 4 | 5 | 6 |
|---|---|---|---|---|---|
| 20–18 | 17–15 | 14–12 | 11–10 | 9–7 | 6–0 |

## Klassenarbeit 1
**Schwerpunkte:** *Listening comprehension, vocabulary, grammar, mediation*

**50 minutes**

**I Listening comprehension: Teenagers at work** (Track 4)

Laura from Philadelphia is being interviewed by a DJ from Radio One. She tells the listeners about the jobs she has already had and the ones she is interested in now.
Listen to the interview and do the tasks.

**A True or false?** (5 pts.)

Mark the right box.

|   | | true | false |
|---|---|---|---|
| 1. | Laura thinks young people should work to earn money. | ☐ | ☐ |
| 2. | Most companies do not want to give jobs to teenagers. | ☐ | ☐ |
| 3. | Teenagers are always late for work. | ☐ | ☐ |
| 4. | Laura enjoyed working in a restaurant because she earned a lot. | ☐ | ☐ |
| 5. | Laura has no hopes of ever getting her dream job. | ☐ | ☐ |

**B Comprehension**

1. Name the jobs Laura has had so far. (3 pts.)

   _____
   _____
   _____

2. Explain why Laura thinks she never gets the right job.
   Write about three sentences. (6 pts.)

   _____
   _____
   _____
   _____
   _____

## C Text production (8 pts.)

Write about the kind of job **you** would like to do to earn some pocket money.
Give at least three reasons for your answer.

## II Vocabulary: British and American English (8 pts.)

Replace the American expressions with their British equivalents.

KAREN: Oh, let's go into that store over there. I really need some new pants. And those colors are so beautiful.

NANCY: Alright, I will just text Ruth on my cell phone to tell her where we are. She's late because there has been a delay on the subway.

KAREN: Well, we could buy some candy and wait in the sunshine until she arrives. Then we could try on clothes together.

NANCY: I don't know. I've just had breakfast. I always get up late on weekends. It feels like I'm on vacation again. What about having a milkshake while we are waiting for Ruth?

## III Grammar

### A Definite or indefinite article: Teenage life (10 pts.)

Put in the definite or indefinite article, but only where necessary.

I think _____ life of most teenagers today is really hard. I'm always in _____ hurry. I hate _____ school. Yesterday I had _____ fever, but I couldn't stay at home because we had to take _____ test. I work at a restaurant two nights _____ week. I know I should go to _____ bed early at _____ weekends. But on _____ Saturday evenings I go to _____ cinema or disco with my friends.

### B Pronouns: A party at the youth club (16 pts.)

Put in the correct pronouns.

DAVID: Where is Matt? I can't see _____.

ROBERT: Matt can't come. _____ fell off _____ bike yesterday and hurt _____.

DAVID: I hurt _____ hand last year when I broke a glass and cut _____ on one of _____ pieces.

CHRIS: Tom and Fred would have liked to come to the party, but when _____ asked _____ parents, they said "no". Most parents are quite liberal, but _____ are really strict.

HELEN: Well, my mum is certainly very strict, too. Did you enjoy _____ at Jane's party last night, Sue? I wasn't allowed to go because of the Maths test.

SUE: Yes, of course. Sally and I met all _____ friends and _____ helped _____ to some nice cakes and sandwiches.

CHRIS: Oh, I've stepped on something. Is this _____ jacket, Pete?

PETE: No, it isn't _____, it's Jack's.

## IV  Mediation: Going shopping (15 pts.)

You are going shopping with some German friends and your English exchange partner. Your exchange partner can understand German quite well, but has problems with some sentences.
Express in English what your German friends are saying.

1. „Die Kleidung bei H&M sieht wirklich nett aus."

2. „Sie hat sich gestern zwei Jeans gekauft."

3. „Ich mag diese Sonnenbrille – wie viel kostet sie?"

4. „Kannst du mir einen Rat geben: Welches Kleid soll ich kaufen?"

5. „Die italienischen Möbel sind toll, aber sie sind zu teuer."

# Solution

**I  Listening comprehension: Teenagers at work (Transcript)**

INTERVIEWER: Welcome to Radio One. Our topic this morning is "Teenagers at work". My guest today is Laura Parker. Hi, Laura, I'd like to ask you a few questions about the jobs you've had. But first tell me: Do you think it's important for teenagers to work?

LAURA: Yes, I think young people should do a lot of different jobs.

INTERVIEWER: To get money?

LAURA: No, for experience.

INTERVIEWER: Is it easy for a teenager to find work?

LAURA: No, not at all. Often you hear that you're not old enough for the job. Most companies want people with experience in the world of work. And then there's the problem of getting there. They ask you if you can drive, if you have a car. They wanna make sure that you can get to work on time.

INTERVIEWER: What kinds of jobs have you had so far?

LAURA: First I worked in a restaurant. It was really hard sometimes, but I enjoyed serving the guests. You get to meet a lot of different people. After that I worked in an office and then in a store.

INTERVIEWER: Do you think these jobs will help you in what you want to do later in life?

LAURA: Yes and no. I know more about different kinds of jobs now, what I like and dislike about them. But on the other hand I didn't really get the job I wanted. I wanted to learn about fashion, but I never got to sell clothes. I never seem to get the right kind of job. There's a lot of discrimination, not only about color, but also looks. Employers are only interested in your age, your looks, your clothes. If you look stylish, you'll get the job.

INTERVIEWER: But can't you dress up, just for the interview?

LAURA: Not if you don't have the clothes or the know-how. If no one around you dresses well, you have no role models; you only have fashion magazines to look at.

INTERVIEWER: Thank you, Laura. We'll be right back after some music ...

A **True or false?**

*Hinweis: Die Aussagen folgen dem Textverlauf. Am besten liest du dir einmal alle Sätze durch, um dir einen Überblick zu verschaffen. Nach dem ersten Durchgang des Hörverstehens solltest du die Aufgabe A möglichst abgeschlossen haben. Dann kannst du dich im zweiten Durchgang ganz auf Aufgabe B konzentrieren. Der Begriff „employer" (a person who gives s.o. a job) könnte für dich neu sein.*

|   |   | true | false |
|---|---|---|---|
| 1. | Laura thinks young people should work to earn money. |   | ✓ |
| 2. | Most companies do not want to give jobs to teenagers. | ✓ |   |
| 3. | Teenagers are always late for work. |   | ✓ |
| 4. | Laura enjoyed working in a restaurant because she earned a lot. |   | ✓ |
| 5. | Laura has no hopes of ever getting her dream job. | ✓ |   |

B **Comprehension**

*Hinweis: Du solltest dir vor dem zweiten Durchgang des Hörverstehens die beiden Aufgabenstellungen durchlesen. Die erste Aufgabe erfordert nur eine Aufzählung, du kannst dich also kurz fassen. Die zweite Aufgabe solltest du in ganzen Sätzen beantworten. Hier machst du dir während des Hörens am besten nur Stichpunkte und formulierst die Aufgabe hinterher genau aus. So verpasst du keine wichtigen Informationen.*

1. Laura has worked at a restaurant, in an office and in a store/shop.
2. Laura would like to work in a job where she can learn about fashion. But employers want people who look good and dress well. Laura doesn't know much about fashion and has only the models in magazines to look at, so she thinks she is not accepted because of her looks. (Laura thinks this is unfair.)

C **Text production**

*Hinweis: Hier gibt es natürlich viele verschiedene Lösungen. Wichtig ist, dass du erklärst, warum dieser Job dir gefällt. Du kannst auch näher beschreiben, was du genau tun willst, wie oft du arbeiten möchtest und wo. Du erhältst 3 Punkte für den Inhalt, 5 Punkte für die Sprache.*

I would like to work as a babysitter for our neighbours. I know their children and they are OK and not too little. So I can play with them while their parents are away. Moreover our neighbours are really nice people who pay quite well and are happy and grateful to have someone to look after their children.

## II Vocabulary: British and American English

KAREN: Oh, let's go into that ~~store~~ over there. I really need some new ~~pants~~. And those ~~colors~~ are so beautiful.　　*shop*
*trousers, colours*

NANCY: Alright, I will just text Ruth on my ~~cell phone~~ to tell her where we are. She's late because there has been a delay on the ~~subway~~.　　*mobile (phone)*
*underground*

KAREN: Well, we could buy some ~~candy~~ and wait in the sunshine until she arrives. Then we could try on clothes together.　　*sweets*

NANCY: I don't know. I've just had breakfast. I always get up late ~~on~~ weekends. It feels like I'm on ~~vacation~~ again. What about having a milkshake while we are waiting for Ruth?　　*at*
*holiday*

## III Grammar

### A Definite or indefinite article: Teenage life

*Hinweis: Beachte, dass du nur dann den bestimmten Artikel verwenden kannst, wenn klar ist, von welchem Nomen du sprichst. In festen Ausdrücken gibt es keine Wahlmöglichkeit.*

I think **the** life of most teenagers today is really hard. I'm always in **a** hurry. I hate **/** school. Yesterday I had **a** fever, but I couldn't stay at home, because we had to take **a** test. I work at a restaurant two nights **a** week. I know I should go to **/** bed early at **the** weekends. But on **/** Saturday evenings I go to **the** cinema or disco with my friends.

### B Pronouns: A party at the youth club

*Hinweis: Bei dieser Übung musst du entscheiden, welche Art von Pronomen in den jeweiligen Zusammenhang passt:*
*– Personalpronomen/personal pronoun (I, you …),*
*– Possessivbegleiter/possessive determiner (my, your …),*
*– Possessivpronomen/possessive pronoun (mine, yours …) oder*
*– Reflexivpronomen/reflexive pronoun (myself, yourself …).*
*Wenn du dir unsicher bist, findest du in der Kurzgrammatik auf den Seiten 5 bis 7 nähere Informationen zu den Pronomen.*

DAVID: Where is Matt? I can't see **him**.

ROBERT: Matt can't come. **He** fell off **his** bike yesterday and hurt **himself**.

DAVID: I hurt **my** hand last year when I broke a glass and cut **myself** on one of **its** pieces.

CHRIS: Tom and Fred would have liked to come to the party, but when **they** asked **their** parents, they said "no". Most parents are quite liberal, but **theirs** are really strict.

HELEN: Well, my mum is certainly very strict, too. Did you enjoy **yourself** at Jane's party last night, Sue? I wasn't allowed to go because of the Maths test.

SUE: Yes, of course. Sally and I met all **our** friends and **we** helped **ourselves** to some nice cakes and sandwiches.

CHRIS: Oh, I've stepped on something. Is this **your** jacket, Pete?

PETE: No, it isn't **mine**, it's Jack's.

## IV Mediation: Going shopping

*Hinweis: Manche Nomen (besonders Sammelbezeichnungen, Paarwörter und bestimmte abstrakte Begriffe) werden im Englischen anders verwendet als im Deutschen. Manchmal verwendet man im Deutschen ein Wort im Singular (z. B. „Kleidung") während im Englischen ein Wort im Plural verwendet werden muss („clothes"). Für jeden Satz erhältst du maximal 3 Punkte.*

1. The clothes at H&M look really nice.
2. Yesterday she bought two pairs of jeans.
3. I like these sunglasses – how much do they cost?
4. Can you give me some/a piece of advice: which dress should I buy?
5. The Italian furniture is great/fantastic, but it is too expensive.

## Notenschlüssel:

| 1 | 2 | 3 | 4 | 5 | 6 |
|---|---|---|---|---|---|
| 71–62 | 61–53 | 52–44 | 43–35 | 34–23 | 22–0 |

> **Klassenarbeit 2**
> **Schwerpunkte:** *Reading comprehension, text production, mediation*

**45 minutes**

## I  Reading comprehension: Pedro leaves school

1  Pedro had not slept very well. When his father banged at the door and shouted: "It's six-thirty – time to get up!" Pedro just turned over and went back to sleep. As usual he had gone to bed late and could sleep forever in the mornings. When he woke up again, it was almost noon.

5  Pedro got up, dressed and went downstairs. His mother was in the kitchen, busy as always, feeding the baby twins. She did not even look up when Pedro came in and sat down at the big, old table. Minutes later she looked up and asked, "Why are you not at school?" Pedro had started eating his breakfast and did not answer. "What's the matter with you? I thought you wanted to finish school to get
10  a better job than your father?" his mother went on.

"I'm leaving school," murmured Pedro, stood up and left the house, not paying attention to his mother's angry voice behind him.

His parents couldn't understand him, he thought. Work and money were the only things they talked about, but they didn't earn enough to be able to afford a
15  better life. Pedro looked around. For the first time he noticed how shabby the houses in his street were. Some of his friends had already left the neighbourhood. Their families had found better places to live. Suddenly Pedro felt depressed and lonely.

He walked down the street, not knowing where to go or what to do. Everybody
20  he knew was at work – or at school. Slowly Pedro walked on, automatically turning towards Main Street with its shops and cheap restaurants. Cars passed, people moved fast without looking at him. He was surrounded by strangers.

But then he saw them: six or seven boys, hanging around in front of the ice-cream parlour. They were members of the Main Street gang – he recognised
25  them at once. Pedro stopped short and turned his back on them. He hoped they hadn't seen him. When he was out in the streets with his friends, he wasn't afraid, and nobody dared to bother them. But today everything was different. Pedro walked away, faster and faster – but then he heard loud voices behind him. They were shouting something and it didn't sound very friendly. Pedro
30  turned around a corner and started to run. There was only one safe place he knew here: the youth club at the end of the street. Pedro heard the shouts coming closer. Out of breath he reached the youth club, threw himself against the door, stumbled and hit the floor inside. Mr Cameron, the social worker, who was sitting at a table near the entrance, looked up and eyed the boy suspiciously.

"Everything OK, Pedro?" he asked, but when Pedro did not answer, he left him alone.

Pedro went to one of the big windows and looked out. The gang had disappeared; the street in front of the club was empty. Pedro waited for some minutes, but there was nobody to be seen. Pedro took a deep breath and went to the pool table. He was on familiar ground now. He would play a game of pool and watch TV. Maybe Andy and José would show up later. They would talk, joke, laugh as usual. Pedro didn't want to worry about the future. Not now, not yet.

*(554 words)*

**A    Multiple matching: Who might have thought this?**  (6 pts.)

Match the following statements to the right person in the story.
Watch out: There are two letters that cannot be matched.

| | | | |
|---|---|---|---|
| 1 | He will talk to me when he is ready. | a | Pedro |
| 2 | I don't understand Pedro. We always did our best to give him a future. | b | Mr Cameron |
| | | c | Pedro's friends at school |
| | | d | Andy and José |
| 3 | Great! Let's have a fight. | e | Pedro's mother |
| 4 | I cannot stand this dirt and depression anymore. | f | Members of the Main Street Gang |
| 5 | I don't have any more time. I need to get to work. | g | Pedro's father |
| | | h | Pedro's twin brothers |
| 6 | Let's go to the youth club later. Maybe Pedro is there. | | |

| 1 | 2 | 3 | 4 | 5 | 6 |
|---|---|---|---|---|---|
|   |   |   |   |   |   |

**B    Multiple choice: How does Pedro feel?**  (4 pts.)

Choose adjectives to describe Pedro's feelings:

Pedro is ...

☐ unhappy.
☐ full of hate.
☐ all by himself.
☐ frightened of the street gang.
☐ afraid of the future.
☐ feeling misunderstood.
☐ happy to be out of school.

C  **Text production** (15 pts.)

Imagine you were in Pedro's position and had to decide if you would rather leave school or stay on.
Give reasons for your decision. Write at least 100 words.

_____
_____
_____
_____
_____

II  **Mediation: At the youth club** (15 pts.)

You are visiting a German youth club together with your American exchange partner Jack. At the door you see a huge poster with the heading "Hausordnung". Jack's German is not very good, so you have to explain to him what the poster is about.
Answer Jack's questions and pay attention to the auxiliaries.

---

### HAUSORDNUNG

Es ist unser Ziel, eine Begegnungsstätte zu schaffen und sinnvolle Freizeitangebote zu machen.

Wenn ihr **mindestens 14 Jahre** alt seid, könnt ihr unseren Klub täglich von **15–21 Uhr** besuchen.

Für euren Aufenthalt im Klub gibt es einige Regeln, die zu eurem eigenen Schutz von euch eingehalten werden müssen:

- Das Mitbringen von Alkohol oder Drogen ist verboten, Rauchen ist auf dem gesamten Gelände nicht gestattet.
- Hunde sind im Klub nicht zugelassen.
- Alle Jugendlichen sind verpflichtet, den Anweisungen der verantwortlichen Aufsichtspersonen Folge zu leisten.
- Spiele, Tischtennisschläger und Bälle können an der Theke ausgeliehen werden.
- Alle Räume sind in ordentlichem Zustand zu hinterlassen. Bitte vermeidet Müll und behandelt Möbel und andere Einrichtungsgegenstände sorgfältig!

JACK: What is this about?
YOU: _____
_____
_____

JACK: I see. The club is open from 3 to 9 p.m. I can understand that. But what does it say at the beginning?
YOU: _____
_____
_____

JACK: The next sentence is about alcohol and drugs, isn't it?
YOU: _____
_____

JACK: And what do they say about dogs?
YOU: _____
_____
_____

JACK: I don't understand what they mean by "Anweisungen der verantwortlichen Aufsichtspersonen Folge zu leisten".
YOU: _____
_____
_____

JACK: I see. You can play games and table tennis here, can't you?
YOU: _____
_____
_____

JACK: There are some more funny words in the next sentence. What does "in ordentlichem Zustand hinterlassen" mean?
YOU: _____
_____
_____

## Solution

## I Reading Comprehension: Pedro leaves school

### A Multiple matching: Who might have thought this?

*Hinweis:* Lies den Text genau durch, um die möglichen Reaktionen und Gedanken der beteiligten Personen besser einschätzen zu können. Vielleicht hilft es dir, im Text Passagen zu unterstreichen, die für die Aufgabe wichtig sind. Wenn du dir nicht sicher bist, welcher Person eine Aussage zugeordnet werden kann, lass diesen Satz offen und mache mit dem nächsten weiter. Am Ende bleiben nur wenige Möglichkeiten offen. Aber achte darauf, dass es auch zwei falsche Lösungen gibt, die du ausschließen musst.

| 1 | 2 | 3 | 4 | 5 | 6 |
|---|---|---|---|---|---|
| b | e | f | a | g | d |

Distraktoren: c, h

### B Multiple choice: How does Pedro feel?

*Hinweis:* Gehe nun den Text nochmals durch. Unterstreiche dir die Stellen, die dir Auskunft über Pedros Gefühle und Charaktereigenschaften geben. Erst dann ist es sinnvoll, die „multiple choice"-Aufgabe zu beantworten. Hier brauchst du den Text noch nicht zu interpretieren, gehe nur von den tatsächlich genannten Fakten aus.

Pedro is …

- [x] unhappy.
- [ ] full of hate.
- [x] all by himself.
- [x] frightened of the street gang.
- [ ] afraid of the future.
- [x] feeling misunderstood.
- [ ] happy to be out of school.

### C Text production

*Hinweis:* Hier sollst du Stellung zu Pedros Entschluss nehmen, die Schule zu verlassen. Achte auf die Hinweise, die du in der Geschichte erhältst und begründe deine Meinung mit Argumenten aus dem Text. Für den Inhalt erhältst du 5, für die Sprache 10 Punkte.

I think I would soon feel bad about not going to school and eventually return. Pedro does not appear to be interested in getting an education, but he obviously feels lonely and aimless as soon as he has decided to leave school. All his friends are working or going to school and so Pedro does not know what to do with all the free time he has got now. It would be the same for me. Furthermore, I believe that my parents would try to persuade me to go back to school because they want me to get a good job after school. Going to university is not a bad idea if you want to earn a lot of money and you need good marks to be able to study. I would stay in school. (135 words)

## II  Mediation: At the youth club

*Hinweis: Du musst hier nur die wichtigsten Punkte der Hausordnung auf Englisch erklären. Für den Inhalt erhältst du 5, für die Sprache 10 Punkte.*

JACK: What is this about?

YOU: It tells you what you can and can't do at the youth club.

JACK: I see. The club is open from 3 to 9 p.m. I can understand that. But what does it say at the beginning?

YOU: It says that the club is a meeting place for young people and offers all kinds of free-time activities.

JACK: The next sentence is about alcohol and drugs, isn't it?

YOU: Yes, you mustn't bring alcohol or drugs with you.

JACK: And what do they say about dogs?

YOU: They say that dogs aren't allowed in the club.

JACK: I don't understand what they mean by „Anweisungen der verantwortlichen Aufsichtspersonen Folge leisten".

YOU: It means that you must do what the social workers tell you.

JACK: I see. You can play games and table tennis here, can't you?

YOU: That's right. You can borrow games, table tennis bats and balls at the desk over there.

JACK: There are some more funny words in the next sentence. What does "in ordentlichem Zustand hinterlassen" mean?

YOU: It means that you must keep the rooms tidy and take your waste/rubbish /trash with you.

## Notenschlüssel:

| 1 | 2 | 3 | 4 | 5 | 6 |
|---|---|---|---|---|---|
| 40–36 | 35–31 | 30–26 | 25–21 | 20–13 | 12–0 |

> **Klassenarbeit 3**
> **Schwerpunkte:** *Listening comprehension, grammar, mediation*

**40 minutes**

I **Listening comprehension: Winton Outback Festival** (Track 5)

Listen to a radio report about a famous festival in the Australian town of Winton and then do the tasks.

A **Multiple choice** (6 pts.)

Tick the right answers.

1. Winton is in …
   - [ ] New South Wales.
   - [ ] Elderslie.
   - [ ] Queensland.
   - [ ] the Northern Territory.

2. "Waltzing Matilda" is …
   - [ ] an Australian film.
   - [ ] a book about Winton.
   - [ ] a famous poem.
   - [ ] an Australian song.

3. The festival takes place …
   - [ ] every other year.
   - [ ] in August.
   - [ ] in September.
   - [ ] every three years.

4. Robin Peters is invited to the radio show as an Outback Festival expert because he …
   - [ ] organises the festival.
   - [ ] is a local.
   - [ ] has participated in many competitions at the Festival.
   - [ ] won last year's "Dunny Derby".

5. The festival events include …
   - [ ] activities for kids.
   - [ ] swimming competitions.
   - [ ] a show of wild Australian animals.
   - [ ] a boat race.

6. During the festival, most people spend the night in …
   - [ ] tents.
   - [ ] the open air.
   - [ ] their car.
   - [ ] private houses.

**B  Explain the following words.** (6 pts.)

1. outback

   _____

   _____

2. "Dunny Race"

   _____

   _____

3. volunteer

   _____

   _____

## II Grammar

### A  Relative clauses (12 pts.)

Make one sentence out of two. Use a relative clause to connect the two parts.

1. Australia is visited by millions of tourists every year.
   It is a fascinating country.

   _____

   _____

2. Tourists travel to the outback.
   They are interested in endless deserts and rock formations.

   _____

   _____

3. Some of them do not take the right equipment with them.
   These people are not well enough informed.

   _____
   _____

4. Ayers Rock is a famous sight.
   Many tourists want to see it.

   _____
   _____

5. The Aborigines have always produced colourful paintings.
   Their works of art are admired by experts.

   _____
   _____

6. Australia has got many beautiful beaches.
   Visitors are enthusiastic about them.

   _____
   _____

## B  Position of adverbs and adverbials (6 pts.)

Put the word order right. Pay attention to adverbs and adverbials.

1. tourists/the Great Barrier Reef/often/in Northeast Australia/visit

   _____
   _____

2. divers and snorkellers/every day/hundreds of/the beauty of the reef/enjoy

   _____
   _____

3. of the reef/tourism/the ecology/unfortunately/can endanger

   _____
   _____

**III  Mediation: The Iron Kids Event at the Winton Outback Festival**  (12 pts.)

You have just started working for the non-profit group that organises the Winton Festival. Today 14-year-old Sven Sandhöfer e-mails you. He has heard about the Iron Kids competition and asks you for some information on the event. Luckily you find the leaflet printed below on your desk.

Sum up the main aspects for Sven in German in about 100 words.

# Let's strike while the iron is hot!

Do you want your child to take part in this year's Iron Kids Event? The fun seems endless with five different contests in three days, challenging your child's artistic and strategic skills.

### Activities include:

- **Bowl-A-Saurus** (bowling)
- **Opal Miners' Dash** (sprinting over a short distance)
- **Swag Toss** (throwing a bundle of clothes as far as you can)
- **Whip Cracking** (loudest sound wins)
- **Tugging a Mini Moke** (pulling the car on the photo as far as possible)

The winner takes it all and will gain fame, a fantastic yellow Iron Kid T-shirt and a geared push bike.
Admission fees run low at only $ 5 per child.
Competitors will face seventeen opponents in their age group.
Children aged 10 to 15 years are welcome to apply.

So don't spoil all the fun for your child and download the admission form at www.outback-ironkids.au!

# Solution

## I Listening comprehension: Winton Outback Festival (Transcript)

*Hinweis:* Lies die Aufgaben genau durch, bevor du den Text zweimal anhörst.
Die Wörter „host" (Gastgeber) und „town council" (Stadtrat) sind vielleicht neu für dich.

ANNOUNCER: Dear listeners, I'm standing here in front of the Visitor Information Centre in Eldersie Street in Winton, Queensland. Winton with its 900 inhabitants is a quiet rural town in the outback. It's mainly known as the birthplace of "Waltzing Matilda", Australia's national song. But every second September the small community is host to the Winton Outback Festival, one of the biggest events in Queensland. The first festival was held in August 1972 and because it was so successful the town council decided to repeat it again in 1973. Since then the festival has become well-known not only in Australia, but internationally as well. The event is known for its special Aussie competitions and relaxed outback atmosphere. I've got Robin Peters here, born and raised in Winton, who will be able to tell us everything about this outstanding festival. Hi, Robin.

ROBIN PETERS: Hi Rebecca, and welcome to Winton.

ANNOUNCER: It's a pleasure to be here. Now, can you tell our listeners a bit about the different competitions and events that make the Winton Outback Festival so special?

ROBIN PETERS: Well, the most important and certainly funniest event is the famous "Australian Dunny Derby" (for all of you who don't speak Australian slang: a dunny is a small outside toilet). 20 teams are invited to build their own movable dunnies and race them over a 250 m track.

ANNOUNCER: That's certainly quite an unusual sporting activity. And what else can visitors expect?

ROBIN PETERS: There are dozens of other exciting competitions, like the Outback Iron Man and Iron Woman event, the Bushman's Egg Throwing Competition, the Country/Rock Music Spectacular and workshops for children, just to name a few of the 50 attractions during the five festival days.

ANNOUNCER: That sounds really great. Where can people stay during the festival? Has Winton got enough hotel and Bed & Breakfast rooms?

ROBIN PETERS: Well, we wouldn't be able to offer enough rooms, but there is a whole tent city with modern tents already built up for the visitors. Each tent sleeps 2 or 3 people and there are hot showers, toilets etc. close by. So bring your sleeping bag and join the happy crowd.

ANNOUNCER: Fantastic! Just one more question: How is it possible to organise such a huge festival with so many events and visitors in a small community like Winton?

ROBIN PETERS: The festival is organised by a non-profit making group with one full-time coordinator and many volunteers who come from all over Australia to help us. Most of them return every year and enjoy the great atmosphere and the chance to make new friends. Volunteers are always welcome and everyone who helps is invited to a big volunteer party at the end of the festival.

ANNOUNCER: Thank you very much, Robin, for the first-hand information. Have a great time at the festival.

**A   Multiple choice**

1. Winton is in …
   - [ ] New South Wales.
   - [ ] Elderslie.
   - [✓] Queensland.
   - [ ] the Northern Territory.

2. "Waltzing Matilda" is …
   - [ ] an Australian film.
   - [ ] a book about Winton.
   - [ ] a famous poem.
   - [✓] an Australian song.

3. The festival takes place …
   - [ ] every other year.
   - [ ] in August.
   - [✓] in September.
   - [ ] every three years.

4. Robin Peters is invited to the radio show as an Outback Festival expert because he …
   - [ ] organises the festival.
   - [✓] is a local.
   - [ ] has participated in many competitions at the Festival.
   - [ ] won last year's "Dunny Derby".

5. The festival events include …
   - [x] activities for kids.
   - [ ] swimming competitions.
   - [ ] a show of wild Australian animals.
   - [ ] a boat race.

6. During the festival most people spend the night in …
   - [x] tents.
   - [ ] the open air.
   - [ ] their car.
   - [ ] private houses.

**B  Explain the following words.**

*Hinweis: Für die Definition des Begriffs „Dunny Race" ist der Kontext des Hörverstehenstexts wichtig. Die anderen beiden Erklärungen kannst du aufgrund deines Hintergrundwissens geben. Zusätzlich kannst du beim zweiten Anhören nach Informationen suchen, die dir bei der Umschreibung der Begriffe helfen.*

1. The outback is a very dry area of land in northwestern Australia where only few people live.
2. The "Dunny Race" is a competition where people have to race toilets on wheels along a 250 m track.
3. A volunteer is a person that agrees to help organise a festival, for example, and does not usually get any money for it.

## II  Grammar

### A  Relative clauses

*Hinweis: Bei dieser Aufgabe solltest du darauf achten, ob es sich um notwendige oder nicht notwendige Relativsätze handelt. Bilde „contact clauses", wo es möglich ist. Wenn es dir schwer fällt, dich an die unterschiedlichen Arten von Relativsätzen zu erinnern, sieh dir die Regeln auf den Seiten 25 und 26 nochmals genau an.*

1. Australia, which is a fascinating country, is visited by millions of tourists every year.
2. Tourists who are interested in endless deserts and rock formations travel to the outback.

3. Some of them, who are not well enough informed, do not take the right equipment with them.
4. Ayers Rock is a famous sight (that/which) many tourists want to see./ Ayers Rock, which many tourists want to see, is a famous sight.
5. The Aborigines, whose works of art are admired by experts, have always produced colourful paintings.
6. Australia has got many beautiful beaches (that/which) visitors are enthusiastic about.

## B Position of adverbs and adverbials

*Hinweis: Wiederhole noch einmal die Regeln zur Wortstellung im Englischen (vgl. S. 22), besonders die Stellung der Adverbien (vgl. S. 5)!*

1. Tourists often visit the Great Barrier Reef in Northeast Australia.
2. Hundreds of divers and snorkellers enjoy the beauty of the reef every day./Every day hundreds of divers and snorkelers …
3. Unfortunately tourism can endanger the ecology of the reef./ Tourism can unfortunately endanger the ecology of the reef.

## III Mediation: The Iron Kids Event at the Winton Outback Festival

*Hinweis: Versuche, möglichst viele für Sven interessante Aspekte aus dem Werbetext aufzugreifen. Unterstreiche dir Schlüsselwörter auf dem Flyer um die wichtigsten Punkte zu erfassen, auch wenn du nicht alles verstehst. Auch wenn du glaubst, schon alle wesentlichen Punkte auf dem Flyer erfasst zu haben, gleiche sie trotzdem nochmals ab, um sicherzustellen, dass du nichts vergessen hast. Dann ordne die Informationen in einer sinnvollen Reihenfolge an. Zum Beispiel solltest du nicht vergessen, wichtige W-Fragen (z. B. Wer darf an welchem Wettbewerb unter welchen Voraussetzungen teilnehmen?) zu beantworten und Informationen zu demselben Aspekt zu bündeln. Denke daran, deine Antwort kurz und knapp zu fassen. Erst nachdem du diesen Schritt gemacht hast, solltest du damit beginnen, deine Antwort an Sven zu schreiben. Für den Inhalt erhältst du jeweils maximal 8 Punkte, für die sprachliche Leistung 4 Punkte.*

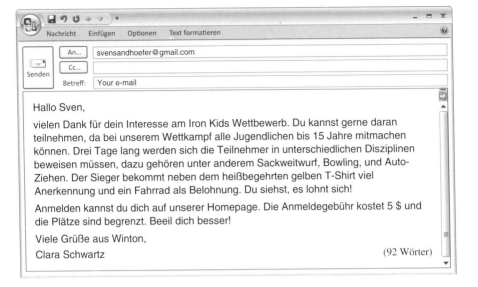

**Notenschlüssel:**

| 1 | 2 | 3 | 4 | 5 | 6 |
|---|---|---|---|---|---|
| 42–37 | 36–31 | 30–26 | 25–21 | 20–14 | 13–0 |

## Klassenarbeit 4
**Schwerpunkte:** *Reading comprehension, mixed grammar, text production*

**50 minutes**

## I Reading comprehension: Youth cultures and music

In the early 1950s Europe was still suffering from the effects of World War II. People were short of food and money and many goods were not available or very expensive. Teenagers lived and dressed like the grown-ups, and there was no separate identity or youth culture. British youth looked towards the USA and
5 those who could afford it tried to copy American idols. The Teddy Boys were the first British youth culture in the 1950s. Young men developed their own dress code and listened to American Rock 'n' Roll, which adults condemned as the "devil's music". Later many young people adopted the "mod" subculture, which centred around modern jazz music, coffee bars, art and Italian fashion.
10 But in the early 1960s more and more bands appeared in the North of England, especially in the industrial cities of Liverpool, Birmingham and Manchester, mixing American Rhythm 'n' Blues and Rock 'n' Roll with their own individual style: the Merseybeat was born.
Four young men, John Lennon, Paul McCartney, George Harrison and Ringo
15 Starr, were just some of the many talented musicians who came together to play in the clubs and halls of Liverpool. But in 1961, The Beatles were discovered by manager Brian Epstein, who was fascinated by the charisma and musical excellence of the band. Two years later The Beatles had succeeded in becoming world-famous, touring the USA and capturing the hearts of teenagers all over the world.
20 "Beatlemania" had arrived. Other groups followed, like The Rolling Stones and The Who. These rock bands became the most influential groups of the 1960s and 1970s in Britain, staying together over the years and inspiring hundreds of other musicians.
As rock music changed British society, young people began to develop their own
25 ideas and values. Earning more money now, they were able to influence the music business and fashion by buying what they liked. So they became an important economic factor. But youth cultures also meant innovation and protest. The rockers, the hippie movement and the punks, who took the scene in the mid-1970s, became dominating forces. Especially the punks fascinated many young people,
30 shocking the older generation with their wild hairstyles and tattoos.
In the 1980s and '90s lifestyle and fashion were again influenced by American music: hard rock and heavy metal, hip hop, techno, but also pop artists like Michael Jackson and Madonna dominated the scene, and MTV and music videos began to have a large effect on the music business.

Today there are no new youth cultures like those in the second half of the 20th century. Generation Z (also known as the Internet Generation), young people all over the world born after the fall of the Soviet Union, have grown up in a time of prosperity and peace. These youngsters can choose from a wide range of lifestyles and cultures. They live in a global village, having access to all kinds of information and entertainment via the World Wide Web and modern media.

*(495 words)*

**A    Multiple matching**　　　　　　　　　　　　　　　　　　　　(5 pts.)

Match the headings with the correct periods of time.

1   1950s　　　　　2   1960s and early '70s

3   mid-1970s　　　4   1980s and '90s

5   21st century

a   Young people depend less on the older generations.

b   American music and Italian fashion influence Europe.

c   The most important musicians of this time come from the South of England.

d   Musicians become famous all over the world because of music channels such as MTV.

e   There is no general youth culture but there are many different possibilities to choose from.

f   Generation Z only cares about computers.

g   English bands attract more and more fans.

| 1 | 2 | 3 | 4 | 5 |
|---|---|---|---|---|
|   |   |   |   |   |

**B  Table completion** (12 pts.)

Look for information in the text and fill in the grid.

|  | 1950s | 1960s/1970s | 1990s |
|---|---|---|---|
| popular music | • <br><br> • | • <br><br> • | • <br><br> • |
| relationship to older generation |  |  |  |
| popular fashion |  |  |  |

**C  Comprehension**

1. Explain why young people have become an "economic factor" (l. 27). (6 pts.)

   _____
   _____
   _____
   _____

2. "Today there are no new youth cultures" (l. 35). Give reasons for this fact. (6 pts.)

   _____
   _____
   _____
   _____

## II  Spot the mistake                                                (10 pts.)

Look at the verb forms and decide whether they are right or wrong.
If you feel they are wrong, correct them.

Tom is always a great fan of rock music. This is
why his girlfriend Ruby has given him a Rolling
Stones concert ticket as a birthday present last
year. Tom was really excited and looked forward
to the concert.

It was a great show. When the Stones arrived on
stage, the fans were already waiting for three
hours. The audience has been told that the tour
bus had had an accident, but the musicians had
not hurt. The Stones are known for their great live
performances and started the concert with some of
their most famous hits. While the band was playing, young and old fans danced wildly.

Tom isn't usually dancing in public, but at the
Stones concert he really enjoyed himself and
cheered with the rest of the crowd.

Next week Tom will go to a Green Day concert.
Cheap tickets have been offered on eBay so he
bought them. He hopes Ruby comes with him.

## III  Text production: The kind of music I like                       (18 pts.)

Choose one kind of music, an artist or a group you like and describe
his/her/its typical features.
Write about 150 words.

## Solution

### I Reading comprehension: Youth cultures and music

#### A Multiple matching

*Hinweis: Lies dir am besten für jeden angegebenen Zeitraum nochmals den entsprechenden Abschnitt im Text durch und überlege, welcher zusammenfassende Überblicksatz sich am besten für diese Textpassage eignet.*

| 1 | 2 | 3 | 4 | 5 |
|---|---|---|---|---|
| b | g | a | d | e |

#### B Table completion

|  | 1950s | 1960s/1970s | 1990s |
|---|---|---|---|
| popular music | • Rock'n'Roll<br>• jazz | • rock<br>• punk<br>(also possible: Hippie music, Merseybeat) | • hard rock<br>• heavy metal<br>(also possible: techno, pop, hip hop) |
| relationship to older generation | teenagers live like grown-ups | teenagers shock the older generation | American lifestyle influences Europe |
| popular fashion | teenagers dress like grown-ups (also possible: Italian fashion) | wild hairstyles, tattoos | American fashion influences Europe (e.g. MTV, culture) |

#### C Comprehension

*Hinweis: Lies den Text sorgfältig und unterstreiche die entsprechenden Passagen, auf die sich die beiden Zitate beziehen. Versuche dann, die Antworten eigenständig zu formulieren.*

1. Young people today earn more money, which they can spend on what they like. So they decide what clothes or music they want to buy. They decide which products the fashion and music business sell best.

2. There are no new youth cultures today because young people all over the world can get information about foreign cultures and styles with the help of TV and the Internet. They can choose from a great number of fashions. Every possible idea seems to be out there already. So there is no reason to develop a new youth culture.

## II  Spot the mistake

> *Hinweis:* Achte bei dieser Aufgabe genau auf den Textzusammenhang, die Wortstellung und die Signalwörter für die Zeiten. Einen Überblick über die Verwendung der Zeiten findest du auf den Seiten 14 bis 22.

Tom ~~is always~~ a great fan of rock music. This is why his girlfriend Ruby ~~has given~~ him a Rolling Stones concert ticket as a birthday present last year. Tom was really excited and looked forward to the concert.

*has always been*
*gave*

It was a great show. When the Stones arrived on stage, the fans ~~were already waiting~~ for three hours. The audience ~~has been told~~ that the tour bus had had an accident, but the musicians ~~had not hurt~~. The Stones are known for their great live performances and started the concert with some of their most famous hits. While the band was playing, young and old fans ~~danced~~ wildly.

*had already been waiting*
*was told / had been told*

*had not been hurt*

*were dancing*

Tom ~~isn't usually dancing~~ in public, but at the Stones concert he really enjoyed himself and cheered with the rest of the crowd.

*doesn't usually dance*

Next week Tom ~~will go~~ to a Green Day concert. Cheap tickets ~~have been~~ offered on eBay, so he bought them. He hopes Ruby ~~comes~~ with him.

*is going to go*
*were*
*will come*

## III  Text production: The kind of music I like

> *Hinweis:* Hier hast du die Freiheit, dich für eine Musikrichtung oder Gruppe zu entscheiden, über die du gut informiert bist. Stelle dir vor, dass der Leser vom Thema nichts oder wenig weiß, und versuche ihn kurz über deine Lieblingsmusik zu informieren. Für den Inhalt des Aufsatzes erhältst du 6, für die Sprache 12 Punkte.

I like listening to Cro. I think he is Germany's most famous rapper at the moment. Actually, his music is somewhere in between pop and rap, which is why he calls it "raop". Cro always wears a Panda mask when he is on stage. This is because he does not want anybody to see his face.

Cro became famous when he published his second mixtape "Meine Musik" on the Internet. Everybody could download it for free. The German hip-hopper Kaas noticed Cro and helped him to find a label. Cro's first album *Raop* was a big success. It was the MTV "Album of the Year 2012".

Cro was called the "Newcomer of the Year" on iTunes and he also won the Bambi Award for "Pop National". You can listen to his most popular songs

"Easy" and "Einmal um die Welt" on the radio almost every day. But Cro can also play the piano and the guitar and he is very successful as a fashion designer, too.

(166 words)

**Notenschlüssel:**

| 1 | 2 | 3 | 4 | 5 | 6 |
|---|---|---|---|---|---|
| 57–50 | 49–42 | 41–35 | 34–28 | 27–19 | 18–0 |

# Klassenarbeit 5
**Schwerpunkte:** *Listening comprehension, English in use, writing an e-mail*

**50 minutes**

**I   Listening comprehension: Britain's Got Talent** (Track 6)

Listen to a conversation between Holly and her father and do the tasks.

**A   True, false? If false, correct the wrong part.** (11 pts.)

            true  false

1. Holly's mum won't be home for dinner.

2. Holly and her father are having a cup of tea before dinner.

3. Holly's father is interested in "Britain's Got Talent".

4. He wants Holly to take part in the show.

5. Mr Wilson wants to give Holly a role in a play.

6. Holly's parents do not like her voice.

7. Holly's mum has to decide if Holly is allowed to take part in the talent show.

**B  Table completion** (6 pts.)

Fill in the grid.

| Reasons why Holly should ... | |
|---|---|
| ... take part in the talent show | ... not take part in the show |
| • | • |
| • | • |
| • | • |

## II  English in use (10 pts.)

Give synonyms or paraphrases for the words/expressions underlined.

HARRY: It's a pity Ethan <u>can't afford</u> to buy an electric guitar. He is such a good musician.

_____

NOAH: And have you heard him sing? He <u>obviously</u> is a talented singer, too.

_____

HARRY: Last time, Ethan had the main part in the school musical. <u>The audience was</u> fascinated by his performance. And the girls nearly went crazy over him.

_____

NOAH: I'm sure he will <u>make a career</u> as a pop star.

_____

HARRY: Well, don't forget <u>to switch</u> the TV on then.

_____

## III Grammar

### A Conditional clauses (10 pts.)

Read the dialogue between Holly and her friend Katie and put in the correct verb forms.

KATIE: If Paul Potts _____ *(not sing)* so well, he _____ *(not/win)* "Britain's Got Talent".

HOLLY: I _____ *(be)* a star now, if I _____ *(have)* the chance to apply.

KATIE: But if you _____ *(not/practise)* enough, you _____ *(not/choose)* by the jury.

HOLLY: Well, my parents don't want to pay for extra singing lessons. I wish I had Lola's parents. If she _____ *(ask)* them for guitar lessons, they _____ *(buy)* her a guitar at once and pay for the teacher. But she isn't even interested in music and has absolutely no talent.

KATIE: I know it's not fair! But wait – here's an idea: I'll ask my older sister – she sings in a band. If she _____ *(agree)* to teach you, you _____ *(be able)* to get enough practice.

HOLLY: Thank you, Katie. You're a great friend.

### B The passive (8 pts.)

Holly's mother tells her daughter a story about the music her parents were crazy about when they were younger.

Change the parts underlined from the active into the passive voice.

MOTHER: (**1**) <u>My parents told me about the hippie movement</u>. It all began in the 1960s. (**2**) At that time <u>people were developing new ways of living</u>. So many young Americans and Europeans travelled to lonesome places and exotic countries. (**3**) <u>They even founded communes</u>.

HOLLY: What was a commune, Mum?

MOTHER: (**4**) That was a place <u>where groups of people shared houses and food</u>. They lived simply because they believed (**5**) <u>man should protect the environment</u>.

HOLLY: Everybody knows that the hippies were peaceful people protesting against weapons and wars. I wish I had been one of them!

MOTHER: Well, it wasn't an easy life, you know. In the 1960s, people were more conservative than today. (**6**) <u>So critics accused the hippies of having a wild and chaotic lifestyle</u>. (**7**) <u>People believed they were stupid</u>. But they just did not understand that peace was more important to the hippies than a good job or expensive clothes. (**8**) And <u>the police watched them</u> wherever they went. So life as a hippie was no piece of cake.

| 1 | |
|---|---|
| 2 | |
| 3 | |
| 4 | |
| 5 | |
| 6 | |
| 7 | |
| 8 | |

## IV Writing an e-mail (15 pts.)

It's Friday evening. You are looking forward to the weekend and have time to write an e-mail to your e-pal in Britain or the US. Tell him/her about your day and a show you have just watched on TV. Write about 150 words.

**Solution**

## I   Listening comprehension: Britain's Got Talent (Transcript)

*Hinweis: „Britain's Got Talent" ähnelt der Talentshow „Deutschland sucht den Superstar", es können sich aber alle Arten von Showtalenten bewerben. Die Vokabeln „to apply" (sich bewerben) und „audition" (Vorsingen) sind vielleicht neu für dich. Lies die Aufgaben zum Hörverständnis genau, bevor du dir den Text zweimal anhörst. Versuche die Aufgabe A während und nach dem ersten Anhören zu bearbeiten. Dann kannst du dich für den zweiten Durchgang auf die Aufgabe B konzentrieren.*

HOLLY: Hi, Dad, I'm back from school.

FATHER: Hi, Holly, everything all right? I've made a nice dinner. Mum's late as usual, but she'll be here in about 20 minutes.

HOLLY: Oh, good. But I'm really hungry. Can I have a cup of tea and a biscuit while we're waiting for her?

FATHER: Of course you can. I've just made a pot of nice, strong tea. It's in the kitchen. Pour yourself a cup. The biscuits are in the box over there.

HOLLY: Thanks. Dad, can we switch on the telly after dinner? "Britain's Got Talent" is on tonight. I'd like to see the new people.

FATHER: OK, we can watch it. It's always interesting to see what kind of talents they present. Do you remember Paul Potts? I think he was really great.

HOLLY: Well, it's not the kind of music I like, but he was very good. I prefer people like George Sampson. By the way, Dad, do you think I could apply for an audition?

FATHER: Oh Holly, is this a joke or are you serious?

HOLLY: Dad, you know I've got a good voice. Didn't I tell you that Mr Wilson said I'll get the main part in the musical he wants to do at school in spring?

FATHER: Of course you're very good and Mum and I are very proud of you. But singing at school and performing in a TV show are two very different things. Didn't you see how unhappy the young people were who applied and weren't chosen?

HOLLY: Dad, I know that there are thousands of teenagers who dream of a career as a pop star. But I'd just like to try it, you see. Maybe I've got a chance. If I don't try, I'll never know.

FATHER: Holly, you're still at school and should concentrate on your exams. You forget it all just because you think you might become famous.

HOLLY: Oh, Dad, I've always been good at school and I promise I'll work hard for my exams. Everybody knows that you can't do without them.

FATHER: I don't know, Holly. But if you're really so keen on having a go, let's ask your mum what she thinks about it. She'll be here in a few minutes. I've just heard her car outside.

**A   True, false? If false, correct the wrong part.**

|   | | true | false |
|---|---|---|---|
| 1. | Holly's mum won't be home for dinner. **Holly's mum will be late for dinner.** | ☐ | ✓ |
| 2. | Holly and her father are having a cup of tea before dinner. | ✓ | ☐ |
| 3. | Holly's father is interested in "Britain's Got Talent". | ✓ | ☐ |
| 4. | He wants Holly to take part in the show. **He doesn't want Holly to take part in the show.** | ☐ | ✓ |
| 5. | Mr Wilson wants to give Holly a role in a play. **Mr Wilson wants to give Holly a role in a musical.** | ☐ | ✓ |
| 6. | Holly's parents do not like her voice. **Holly's parents think she has got a very good voice.** | ☐ | ✓ |
| 7. | Holly's mum has to decide if Holly is allowed to take part in the talent show. | ✓ | ☐ |

**B   Table completion**

*Hinweis:* Hier musst du die Argumente, die für und gegen Hollys Bewerbung bei der Talentshow sprechen, aus dem Hörtext zusammenfassen. Du brauchst keine ganzen Sätze zu schreiben, Stichpunkte reichen völlig aus.

| Reasons why Holly should ... | |
|---|---|
| ... take part in the talent show | ... not take part in the show |
| • good voice<br>• experience in performing on stage because of the main part in the school musical in spring<br>• good at school anyway so the talent show will do no harm to her career | • impossible to compare singing in school and auditioning for a casting show<br>• difficult to be successful in a casting show (too many people apply)<br>• important exams at school |

## II English in use

*Hinweis: Versuche den Sinn der jeweiligen Wendung mit einfachen Worten wiederzugeben, wenn dir kein passendes Synonym einfällt.*

HARRY: It's a pity Ethan **hasn't got enough money** to buy an electric guitar. He is such a good musician.

NOAH: And have you heard him sing? **It's clear that** he is a talented singer, too.

HARRY: Last time, Ethan had the main part in the school musical. **The people who were watching were/the crowd was** fascinated by his performance. And the girls nearly went crazy over him.

NOAH: I'm sure he will **become successful and famous** as a pop star.

HARRY: Well, don't forget **to turn** the TV on then.

## III Grammar

### A Conditional clauses

*Hinweis: Die Aufgabe enthält alle drei Grundtypen von „if-clauses" (auch „mixed types"). Achte deshalb genau auf den Sinn der Aussagen und formuliere den Satz auf Deutsch, wenn du dir unsicher bist. Wenn dir die Bildung der Zeiten in Konditionalsätzen schwer fällt, wiederhole die Regeln auf den Seiten 23 und 24.*

KATIE: If Paul Potts **had not sung** so well, he **wouldn't/would not have won** "Britain's Got Talent".

HOLLY: I **would be** a star now, if I **had had** the chance to apply.

KATIE: But if you **do not/don't practise** enough, you **will not/won't be chosen** by the jury.

HOLLY: Well, my parents don't want to pay for extra singing lessons. I wish I had Lola's parents. If she **asked** them for guitar lessons, they **would buy** her a guitar at once and pay for the teacher. But she isn't even interested in music and has absolutely no talent.

KATIE: I know it's not fair! But wait – here's an idea: I'll ask my older sister – she sings in a band. If she **agrees** to teach you, you **will/'ll be able** to get enough practice.

HOLLY: Thank you, Katie. You're a great friend.

## B  The passive

*Hinweis:* Bei der Umwandlung ins Passiv musst du entscheiden, ob der „by-agent" für das Verständnis des Satzes notwendig ist. Achte auch darauf, dass du die Zeitform beibehältst. Wenn du mit der Bildung der Passivformen noch Probleme hast, lies dazu die Regeln auf den Seiten 21 und 22! Für jede richtig umgewandelte Form erhältst du 2 Punkte.

| 1 | I was told about the hippie movement by my parents. |
|---|---|
| 2 | … new ways of living were being developed. |
| 3 | Even communes were founded (by them). |
| 4 | … where houses and food were shared by groups of people. |
| 5 | … the environment should be protected. |
| 6 | The hippies were accused of having a wild and chaotic lifestyle. |
| 7 | They were believed to be stupid. |
| 8 | … they were watched by the police … |

## IV  Writing an e-mail

*Hinweis:* Bevor du anfängst zu schreiben, überlege dir, welche Informationen für den Adressaten interessant sein könnten. Stelle deine Erlebnisse so dar, dass auch jemand, der deinen Tag nicht miterlebt hat, ihn sich gut vorstellen kann. Vergiss auch nicht, einen Begrüßungssatz und einen passenden Schluss zu formulieren. Du bekommst 5 Punkte für den Inhalt und 10 Punkte für die Sprache.

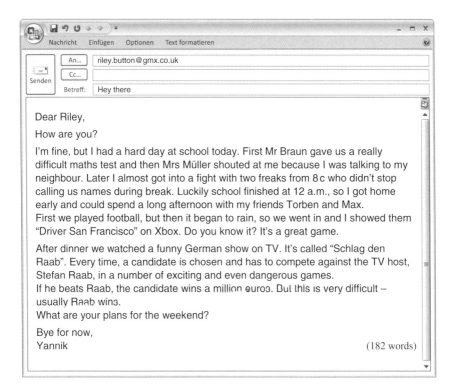

## Notenschlüssel:

| 1 | 2 | 3 | 4 | 5 | 6 |
|---|---|---|---|---|---|
| 60–53 | 52–45 | 44–37 | 36–30 | 29–20 | 19–0 |

## Klassenarbeit 6
### Schwerpunkte: *Mediation, grammar, creative writing*

**45 minutes**

**I   Mediation: Jamestown** (18 pts.)

You and your family are visiting Jamestown, the first English colony in America. They have got a leaflet with all the necessary information, but it is in English, of course.
Read the text carefully and answer your parents' questions.

### The history of Jamestown

Jamestown was America's first permanent colony. It was founded in 1607, 13 years before the Pilgrim Fathers arrived in Massachusetts. Three ships, carrying 105 passengers, left England in December 1606 and reached Virginia in late April 1607. The expedition was paid for by the Virginia Company of London, a group of businessmen that hoped for the discovery of gold and silver in the "New World".

The settlers chose a spot on the James River for its good anchorage and safe position and started to build a camp. Despite the leadership of Captain John Smith, the settlers had serious problems in the early years. Relations to the Powhatan Indians were difficult. An unfamiliar climate as well as the brackish water supply and shortage of food led to illnesses and death. But with the help of Dutch and Polish workmen and the introduction of a new type of tobacco that could be exported, the financial situation of the colony improved. When colonist John Rolfe married Pocahontas, the daughter of a Powhatan chief, a period of peace followed.

Today you can visit the rebuilt settlement. Get on board the three Pilgrim ships, explore James Fort, see the Powhatan Indian Village and experience daily life in the early 17th century.
**Ask for an audio guide at the information desk to find out more about the Pilgrims' fascinating life.**

YOUR FATHER: Warum ist diese Siedlung so wichtig, dass man sie wieder aufgebaut hat?

YOU: _____

_____

_____

YOUR MOTHER: Warum sind die Siedler denn überhaupt nach Virginia gekommen?

YOU: _____

_____

_____

YOUR FATHER: Warum haben sie die Kolonie hier gegründet?

YOU: _____

_____

_____

YOUR MOTHER: Wovon haben die Siedler hier gelebt?

YOU: _____

_____

_____

YOUR MOTHER: Gab es Probleme mit den Indianern?

YOU: _____

_____

_____

YOUR FATHER: Was kann man heute in Jamestown sehen und erleben?

YOU: _____

_____

_____

## II  Grammar: Reported speech (15 pts.)

One of the guides at Jamestown Settlement is telling you and your family about Pocahontas, the Powhatan girl who married colonist John Rolfe. Your little sister Carolin is very interested:

GUIDE: Pocahontas is one of the most fascinating figures of Jamestown history. Historians say they don't know much about her early life, but she is mentioned in a book by John Smith.

CAROLIN: Is it true that she saved the captain's life, Sir?

GUIDE: We are not quite sure about that. We had some experts here last month who think John Smith invented the story later. But have you heard that Pocahontas married a colonist and traveled to England with her husband?

CAROLIN: Yes, and I know about her early death there. But people around the world will always remember Pocahontas as the main character of the famous Disney film.

GUIDE: Come with me to have a look at the rebuilt Powhatan village if you want to see how Pocahontas really lived. I'm going to show you the Indian houses and you will learn about their food, tools and culture.

Later that day, Carolin wants to tell some American friends what she has learned about Pocahontas. But Carolin does not know how to say what she was told in reported speech, so you need to help her.
Use different suitable introductory verbs.

You can start like this:
The guide …

### III Creative writing: A letter from Jamestown (21 pts.)

Imagine you are a settler who arrived in Jamestown on one of the first ships. Write a letter of about 200 words to a friend back in England. Tell him/her about your trip to America and the problems you had during the journey and in the new country.

**Solution**

**I  Mediation: Jamestown**

*Hinweis: Suche im Text die passenden Informationen, um die Fragen zu beantworten. Du brauchst die Sätze nicht wörtlich zu übersetzen, aber die wichtigsten Informationen sollten enthalten sein. Pro Frage erhältst du maximal 3 Punkte für die richtige Antwort.*

YOUR FATHER: Warum ist diese Siedlung so wichtig, dass man sie wieder aufgebaut hat?

YOU: Jamestown war die erste dauerhaft besiedelte englische Kolonie in Amerika.

YOUR MOTHER: Warum sind die Siedler denn überhaupt nach Virginia gekommen?

YOU: Sie wurden von der Virginia Company aus London hierher geschickt. Die Geschäftsleute hofften, dass die Siedler hier Gold und Silber finden.

YOUR FATHER: Warum haben sie die Kolonie hier gegründet?

YOU: Die Schiffe konnten an dieser Stelle gut anlegen und es war ein sicherer Platz um sich niederzulassen.

YOUR MOTHER: Wovon haben die Siedler hier gelebt?

YOU: Zuerst war das Leben sehr hart, weil man keine Schätze fand und es wenig zu essen gab. Dann aber wurde Tabak angebaut, den man gut exportieren konnte. Damit haben die Siedler dann Geld verdient.

YOUR MOTHER: Gab es Probleme mit den Indianern?

YOU: Am Anfang war das Verhältnis zu den Indianern schon schwierig. Als aber der Siedler John Rolfe die Häuptlingstochter Pocahontas heiratete, herrschte einige Jahre Frieden mit den Indianern.

YOUR FATHER: Was kann man heute in Jamestown sehen und erleben?

YOU: Man kann die alten Schiffe, das Fort und das Indianerdorf sehen und entdecken, wie das Leben im 17. Jahrhundert hier war.

**II  Grammar: Reported speech**

*Hinweis: Versuche, unterschiedliche passende Verben zur Einleitung der Sätze zu verwenden. Zudem solltest du auf die richtige Zeitform achten. Beachte auch die Veränderung der Pronomen: Du erzählst die Geschichte jetzt aus deiner eigenen Sicht, nicht aus Carolins. Weitere wichtige Regeln zur indirekten Rede findest du auf den Seiten 27 und 28. Für jeden Satz, in dem die Angleichungen für die indirekte Rede richtig vorgenommen wurden gibt es 1 Punkt, für jedes richtige einleitende Verb einen halben Punkt.*

The guide **told us** that Pocahontas **was** one of the most fascinating figures of Jamestown history. He **explained** that historians **said they didn't know** much about her early life, but that she **was mentioned** in a book by John Smith. Carolin **asked if** it **was** true that Pocahontas **had saved** the captain's life. The guide **answered** that **they weren't** quite **sure** about that. He **mentioned** that **they had had** some experts there **the month before** who **thought** John Smith **had invented** the story later. Then the guide **asked us if we had heard** that Pocahontas **had married** a colonist and **traveled** to England with her husband. Carolin **answered** that **she knew** about that and Pocahontas' early death there. Then **she added** that people around the world **would** always remember Pocahontas as the main character of the famous Disney film. The guide **told us to come** with **him** to have a look at the rebuilt Powhatan village **if we wanted to see** how Pocahontas **had** really **lived**. He **said he was going to show us** the Indian houses and that **we would learn** about their food, tools and culture.

### III Creative Writing: A letter from Jamestown

*Hinweis: Stelle dir vor, du bist ein Siedler aus dem 17. Jahrhundert. Überlege, welche Informationen aus Jamestown für deinen Freund zu Hause interessant sind. Du kannst einige Ideen aus dem Werbeprospekt zu Jamestown übernehmen. Verwende aber nicht die abgedruckten Formulierungen, sondern deine eigenen Worte. Achte zudem auf einen passenden Anfang und Schluss: Beispielsweise hat ein Siedler vor fast 400 Jahren seinen Brief auf keinen Fall mit „Hi!" oder „Hallo" begonnen. Für den Inhalt erhältst du maximal 7, für die Sprache 14 Punkte.*

---

Dear James,

How are you? I often think of you and my parents at home in England and remember the good times we had together. Life here in Virginia is very different from the life I led in our little town.

But first I must tell you about our journey to America. I'm sure you can't imagine how long it was. It took us five months to get here! Food and water on the ship were quite bad and people suffered from strange illnesses. I was sick most of the time because the sea was so rough and there were terrible storms.

When we reached the coast of Virginia, we sailed up a river until we found a safe place to build a camp. We soon met some Indians who threatened to kill us but we gave them some of the goods we had brought with us.

*Since then we have built a strong fort to protect ourselves from attacks. Life here is very hard - we have to work all day and sometimes there isn't enough food or clean water. We haven't found any gold or silver yet, but I still hope for a better future. Maybe we will become rich one day and make lots of money here in America.*

*Take care of yourself.*

*Yours,*
*William*

(226 words)

## Notenschlüssel:

| 1 | 2 | 3 | 4 | 5 | 6 |
|---|---|---|---|---|---|
| 54–48 | 47–41 | 40–34 | 33–27 | 26–18 | 17–0 |

> **Klassenarbeit 7**
> **Schwerpunkte:** *Listening comprehension, English in use, picture task*

**50 minutes**

**I  Listening comprehension: Protecting the environment** (Track 7)

Joshua Miller, who works for the US school magazine "Chicago Cracker", is interviewing two students, Grace and Samuel, about how to protect the environment.
Listen to the interview and do the tasks.

**A  Multiple choice: What are they worried about?** (5 pts.)
Tick the correct box.

|  | waste in the sea | climate change | growing deserts | pollution by oil | future of mankind |
|---|---|---|---|---|---|
| Grace | ☐ | ☐ | ☐ | ☐ | ☐ |
| Samuel | ☐ | ☐ | ☐ | ☐ | ☐ |

**B  Comprehension: Short answers** (6 pts.)
Answer the questions in one to six words.

1. What kind of area is the "Great Pacific Garbage Patch"?
   _____

2. What does Samuel do to reduce environmental pollution?
   _____

3. What are politicians interested in according to Grace?
   **(2 aspects)**
   _____
   _____

4. What should the government spend more money on?
   _____

5. What does Samuel want to use when he is grown up?
   _____

C **Creative writing** (18 pts.)

Imagine that you work on the school magazine with Joshua Miller. Unfortunately, Joshua falls ill and you have to write the article on how to protect the environment. Your work can be based on Joshua's interview.

Write at least 150 words including six different suggestions about how to save the environment.

II **English in use: Adjectives or adverbs?** (12 pts.)

Put in the correct English forms of the German words in brackets.

1. Chemical waste can be _____ (hoch/giftig), but _____ (gefährlich) waste is produced by nuclear power stations.

2. The cars of the future will be _____ (sauber) our cars today. But many people cannot buy a new car. A modern car is _____ (viel/teuer) an old one.

3. Young people in Germany are _____ (besorgt) about environmental pollution, but only _____ (wenig) of them join organisations like Greenpeace.

4. People in industrial countries should not eat so _____ (viel) meat. Vegetables taste _____ (gut) and cost _____ (wenig) meat.

5. Many animals are in danger because rain forests are disappearing _____ (schnell) ever before.

6. We must tell people _____ (höflich) possible what they can do to protect the environment. They won't listen if you talk to them _____ (unfreundlich).

## III Picture task: Analysing a cartoon

1. Look at the cartoon and describe what you can see. (6 pts.)

_____
_____
_____
_____
_____
_____
_____

2. Explain the message of the cartoon. (6 pts.)

# Solution

## I Listening comprehension: Protecting the environment (Transcript)

*Hinweis: Der Hörtext enthält einige spezielle Vokabeln aus dem Bereich Umwelt, die meisten kannst du aber gut aufgrund deines Hintergrundwissens erschließen. Lies die Aufgaben genau durch, und höre dir den Text mindestens zweimal an, um die Einzelheiten zu verstehen. Es ist besser, wenn du dich beim ersten Anhören auf die Aufgabe A konzentrierst und dich bei der zweiten Begegnung mit dem Hörtext ganz der Aufgabe B widmest.*

JOSHUA: Hi, Grace and Samuel, I've heard that you're environmental activists. I'd like to write an article for our school magazine. Can I ask you a few questions on how you feel about environmental protection?

GRACE: Yes, of course. What would you like to know?

JOSHUA: My first question is: What environmental problems are you worried about?

SAMUEL: Well, I'm worried about the increasing pollution of the oceans. Have you heard of the "Great Pacific Garbage Patch"? It's a huge area of the sea which is polluted by waste like plastic and chemicals. And it's growing all the time. It's dangerous for the animals living in the sea.

GRACE: I think changes in the world climate are the most dangerous worrying things for all of us. Deserts are getting bigger, even in our country, and yet we still have terrible storms and floods that destroy whole regions and kill many people.

JOSHUA: And what do you personally do to reduce environmental pollution?

SAMUEL: I think recycling is very important. Look at all the waste our society produces.

GRACE: My friends and I work together. We tell our parents and relatives they should try to save energy and water. Everybody can help to reduce pollution and waste.

JOSHUA: Do you think the government should do more to protect the environment?

GRACE: I believe most politicians are more interested in technological progress and the economy than in the environment.

SAMUEL: The government supports oil production, which pollutes the oceans, and doesn't spend enough money on protecting national parks and forests. I think our politicians could do much more to save nature.

JOSHUA: Let's have a look at the future. What do you wanna do when you are older to reduce environmental pollution?

SAMUEL: I would try to use public transport as much as possible. And I would like to work in a field where alternative sources of energy are explored and developed.

GRACE: I really wonder what life will be like for our children. We have everything we want now. Probably our society will have to learn to lead a simpler life to reduce pollution and waste. But we must start now if we wanna solve the problems of the future.

JOSHUA: Thank you very much for the interview.

**A  Multiple choice: What are they worried about?**

|  | waste in the sea | climate change | growing deserts | pollution by oil | future of mankind |
|---|---|---|---|---|---|
| Grace | ☐ | ✓ | ✓ | ☐ | ✓ |
| Samuel | ✓ | ☐ | ☐ | ✓ | ☐ |

**B  Comprehension: Short answers**

1. a polluted place in the sea
2. recycling
3. technological progress, (the) economy
4. protecting national parks and forests
5. public transport

**C  Creative writing**

*Hinweis: Der Artikel für die Schülerzeitung sollte wie jeder Aufsatz aus Einleitung, Hauptteil und Schluss bestehen. Überlege dir, wie man bereits am Anfang des Textes das Interesse der Leser wecken kann. Vergiss nicht, Tipps zum Umweltschutz zu geben. Der Schluss könnte einen Appell zum Mitmachen enthalten. Für den Inhalt erhältst du 6, für die Sprache 12 Punkte.*

**How you can save the environment**

Many people today are worried about the environment. Waste, air pollution, the danger to nature and the changing climate are big problems. But everyone can help to protect the environment – step by step.

So here are some ideas of what you can do:
- Recycle paper, glass, metal and plastic materials and buy recycled paper to save the trees.
- Take your old clothes to charity shops. That way you can avoid waste and help people in need.

There are also many ways of saving energy:
- Switch off lights when you leave a room that is not in use.
- Do not waste (hot) water.
- Make sure that you do not leave the heating on when the window is open.
- And finally: Don't use the car for short trips. Walk or go by bike. This is better for your health, you can avoid air pollution and you save money and fuel.

Tell your friends and family to do the same. If we all work together, we'll be able to save the environment.

(169 words)

## II English in use: Adjectives or adverbs?

*Hinweis: Bei dieser Aufgabe solltest du nicht nur die Entscheidung „Adjektiv oder Adverb?" treffen, sondern auch die passende Steigerungsform einsetzen, wenn das nötig ist. Achte dabei nicht nur auf geeignete Adjektiv oder Adverbformen, sondern auch auf Formulierungen wie „as ... as", „more ... than" etc. Nähere Informationen findest du in der Kurzgrammatik auf Seite 1 bis 4.*

1. Chemical waste can be **highly poisonous/toxic**, but **the most dangerous** waste is produced by nuclear power stations.

2. The cars of the future will be **cleaner than** our cars today. But many people cannot buy a new car. A modern car is **much more expensive than** an old one.

3. Young people in Germany are **worried/concerned** about environmental pollution, but only **few** of them join organisations like Greenpeace.

4. People in industrial countries should not eat so **much** meat. Vegetables taste **good/better** and cost **less than** meat.

5. Many animals are in danger because rain forests are disappearing **faster than** ever before.

6. We must tell people **as politely as** possible what they can do to protect the environment. They won't listen if you talk to them **rudely/in an unfriendly way**.

## III Picture task: Analysing a cartoon

*Hinweis: Beschreibe den Cartoon möglichst genau. Achte dabei auf passende Redewendungen wie „in the (centre of the) picture", „in the foreground", „in the background", „on the left/right". Konzentriere dich auf Einzelheiten, die den Cartoon ungewöhnlich erscheinen lassen und die im Gegensatz zu deiner Erfahrungswelt stehen. Oft ist hier die tiefere Botschaft des Zeichners versteckt. Es ist hilfreich, wenn du den Titel des Cartoons in deine Überlegungen einbeziehst.*

1. In the picture you can see a road with a car in the background which is driving really fast. It has just run over a ball that looks like the Earth because it has the outline of the continents on it. The ball is quite flat in the middle now and seems to be badly damaged.

2. The cartoon is called "Roadkill". Usually, animals are run over and killed by a car. Here it is not an animal that has been killed but our planet Earth: Of course, the Earth has not really been run over. But too many cars cause too much traffic. This pollutes the air and many people do not even care about the damage they are doing to the Earth. In the end, the Earth and all life on it will die because of the dirt and bad air that cars produce.

**Notenschlüssel:**

| 1 | 2 | 3 | 4 | 5 | 6 |
|---|---|---|---|---|---|
| 53–47 | 46–40 | 39–33 | 32–26 | 25–18 | 17–0 |

# Klassenarbeit 8
### Schwerpunkte: *Reading comprehension, grammar, mediation*

**50 minutes**

## I  Reading comprehension: Queen Elizabeth I

Elizabeth Tudor, the daughter of King Henry VIII and his second wife Anne Boleyn, was born in Greenwich near London in 1533. Her childhood was overshadowed because her mother was
5  executed and her father married again four times. Still, Elizabeth grew up to become the most famous queen of England. She was well looked after by Catherine Parr, the sixth and last of her father's wives, and given the best education. She learnt five
10 languages and became an excellent musician.
When her half-sister Mary came to the throne of England in 1553, Elizabeth's life was in danger because Mary hated her as a rival and had so many Protestants executed that she was called "Bloody Mary". After Mary's early
15 death in 1558 Elizabeth was asked to become the new queen and soon won the hearts of the English. From the very beginning of her reign she travelled through the country to impress people with her personality.
As a woman, Elizabeth had many difficulties to overcome: her ministers tried to influence her, and the French king and a lot of men of the court wanted to marry
20 her. However, Elizabeth, with her knowledge and intelligence, made her own decisions and chose to stay unmarried. In a famous speech she told her soldiers: "I have the body of a weak and feeble[1] woman, but I have the heart and stomach[2] of a king, and of a king of England, too."
Her reign was a time when foreign countries were explored and many discov-
25 eries were made in the field of science. The English sailors combined the love of their homeland with profit: they went on expeditions around the world and took everything valuable home with them. They even attacked Spanish and Portuguese ships. That was when King Philip II of Spain took his chance. He was angry about both the sunken ships and the execution of Mary Stuart, Elizabeth's
30 Catholic rival. King Philip assembled the huge Spanish Armada to wipe out the English ships and invade the country in 1588. However, under the command of Lord Howard of Effingham, the English sent eight burning ships against the enemy and attacked the Spanish with their guns and their small, fast ships. A storm hit the fleeing Spanish survivors, and about sixty-three of their ships and

35 twenty thousand men were lost. The English celebrated, and their success was seen as a victory of the Protestant faith[3]. However, the later years brought new difficulties for Elizabeth: the conflicts with Spain and Ireland did not end, and the English suffered from hunger and the never-ending wars and became unhappy with their queen.

40 Elizabeth died in March 1603, after forty-five years on the English throne. Under her rule England had become famous for its achievements[4] in science and music, and the people had become proud of their country. She was also a great fan of William Shakespeare and supported him. So the time of Queen Elizabeth I will always be remembered as the "Golden Age". *(497 words)*

**Annotations**
1 feeble – weak, not strong
2 stomach – courage
3 faith – belief
4 achievements – success *(Leistungen)*

**A English in use** (12 pts.)

Replace the underlined part of the sentence with your own words.

1. Her childhood <u>was overshadowed</u> because her mother was executed (ll. 3–5):

   _____

2. She was well <u>looked after</u> by Catherine Parr (ll. 7/8):

   _____

3. Mary <u>came to the throne</u> of England in 1553 (ll. 11/12):

   _____

4. <u>From the very beginning of her reign</u> she travelled through the country (ll. 16/17):

   _____

5. King Philip assembled the huge Spanish Armada <u>to wipe out</u> the English ships (ll. 30/31):

   _____

6. The English <u>suffered from hunger</u> (l. 38):

   _____

**B  Multiple choice** (4 pts.)

Tick the right answers.

1. Elizabeth had a difficult time before she became queen as …
   - [ ] her sister Mary was afraid of her and wanted to kill her.
   - [ ] many important men wanted to marry her.
   - [ ] her father did not like her.
   - [ ] she lost her father when she was still very young.

2. The Spanish king attacked England because …
   - [ ] he was jealous of the English success.
   - [ ] English ships destroyed many Spanish ships.
   - [ ] Elizabeth had given the order to execute his wife Mary.
   - [ ] he was very poor and needed more money.

3. The English were able to beat the Spanish Armada because …
   - [ ] they hid behind rocks and surprised the Spanish.
   - [ ] they had huge but very fast ships.
   - [ ] they had more ships than the Spanish.
   - [ ] a storm helped them to beat the Spanish.

4. The time of Queen Elizabeth is called "The Golden Age" because …
   - [ ] England became immensely rich.
   - [ ] the English felt good about their home country.
   - [ ] for the first time everybody had enough to eat.
   - [ ] there was no progress in science, music and literature.

## II  Grammar: Gerund or infinitive? (15 pts.)

Put in the correct forms of the verbs and add a preposition where necessary.

**Two Americans in Stratford-upon-Avon**

Last summer Logan and Andrew, two American students, went on a tour of Europe. Both were looking forward _____ *(spend)* a few days in Stratford-upon-Avon.

While Logan was keen _____ *(see)* Shakespeare's birthplace, Andrew wanted _____ *(go)* to a performance at the

Shakespeare Memorial Theatre. But they hadn't imagined _____ *(be)* surrounded by thousands of other tourists. Soon they were not interested _____ *(walk)* around the crowded streets anymore and decided _____ *(look)* for a place to stay. But it wasn't easy _____ *(find)* a place to sleep. First they went to the tourist information, which was famous _____ *(help)* tourists with their problems. There the nice lady at the desk told them that it was very difficult _____ *(get)* a room at that time of the year without _____ *(book)* a long time before the holiday. After _____ *(phone)* a few hotels, she said there was no place to stay. So she suggested _____ *(leave)* Stratford in the evening. The young men were really worried _____ *(find)* a hostel by then, but they did not give up. Finally, they got a small, expensive room in a Bed & Breakfast place about half a mile from the town centre.

_____ *(visit)* Stratford is a fantastic idea, but you must avoid _____ *(go)* there in the summer.

## III Mediation: Two Americans in Salzburg (15 pts.)

You are staying at the same Bed & Breakfast place as Logan and Andrew. The next evening, the boys want to fly to Salzburg in Austria and stay there for a weekend. Unfortunately, the tourist information sent them a German leaflet, which they cannot understand.

So you have a look at the brochure (on the next page) to tell Andrew and Logan more about …

- the sights that are recommended in the brochure.
- where there are any summer specials in town.
- traditional food in Salzburg.
- how to find youth hostels.

# SALZBURG – DAS GEHT SICH AUS!

Du bist jung und unternehmungslustig, aber fast pleite?
Dann haben wir das perfekte Salzburg-Programm für dich!
Wir stellen dir die wichtigsten Sehenswürdigkeiten der viertgrößten
Stadt Österreichs vor und das alles zu absolut erschwinglichen Preisen.

## EINEN AUSFLUG WERT:

+ **Festung Hohensalzberg:**
Die Burg ist eine der größten Europas und stammt aus dem 11. Jahrhundert. Von oben hat man einen spektakulären Blick über die Stadt. Vor allem abends ist die Aussicht sehr zu empfehlen.

> Mit der **SB-Card** kann man bequem mit der Festungsbahn fahren und spart auch noch Geld.

+ **Bummel durch die historische Altstadt:**
Vorbei am Elternhaus von Wolfgang Amadeus Mozart – wer den Eintrittspreis scheut, kann die Fassade und die kleinen Gassen auf sich wirken lassen.

+ **Süßigkeiten:** klassische Mozartkugeln, Sachertorte oder zahlreiche Kaffeespezialitäten – natürlich mit Schlagobers!

## SAISONALES:

+ **Festspiele:** Für Fans von Konzerten, Opern und Schauspielerei. Für den Minigeldbeutel gibt's die Straßenkünstler, die für wenig Geld tolle Unterhaltung bieten.

> Den ganzen Sommer über

+ **Salzburger Christkindlmarkt:**
Wer hier nicht in Weihnachtsstimmung kommt, dem ist nicht zu helfen: Hier gibt's Spielzeug, Auftritte der berühmten Salzburger Chöre, Glühwein, süßes und herzhaftes Essen.

> Immer im Dezember

## SCHLAFPLÄTZE:
Einfach reinklicken und reservieren unter **jugendherbergsnetz@salzburg.at**

## Solution

**I  Reading comprehension: Queen Elizabeth I**

**A  English in use**

*Hinweis: Hier kannst du dein Ausdrucksvermögen testen. Suche die Ausdrücke, die du ersetzen sollst, im Text und versuche Umschreibungen zu finden, die in den Kontext passen. Für jeden richtig ersetzten Ausdruck bekommst du 2 Punkte.*

1. Her childhood **was quite sad** because her mother was executed.
2. She was well **cared for** by Catherine Parr.
3. Mary **became queen** of England in 1553.
4. **After she became queen** she travelled through the country.
5. King Philip assembled the huge Spanish Armada to **defeat / beat / destroy** the English ships.
6. The English **didn't have enough to eat**.

**B  Multiple choice**

*Hinweis: Lies den Text nochmal genau durch und markiere die Stellen, auf die sich die Aufgabe bezieht. Sieh dir in jedem Fall die vorgeschlagenen Lösungen genau an, damit du kein entscheidendes Detail übersiehst.*

1. Elizabeth had a difficult time before she became queen as …
   - [✓] her sister Mary was afraid of her and wanted to kill her.
   - [ ] many important men wanted to marry her.
   - [ ] her father did not like her.
   - [ ] she lost her father when she was still very young.

2. The Spanish king attacked England because …
   - [ ] he was jealous of the English success.
   - [✓] English ships destroyed many Spanish ships.
   - [ ] Elizabeth had given the order to execute his wife Mary.
   - [ ] he was very poor and needed more money.

3. The English were able to beat the Spanish Armada because …
   - [ ] they hid behind rocks and surprised the Spanish.
   - [ ] they had huge but very fast ships.
   - [ ] they had more ships than the Spanish.
   - [✓] a storm helped them to beat the Spanish.

4. The time of Queen Elizabeth is called "The Golden Age" because …
- [ ] England became immensely rich.
- [✓] the English felt good about their home country.
- [ ] for the first time everybody had enough to eat.
- [ ] there was no progress in science, music and literature.

## II Grammar: Gerund or infinitive?

*Hinweis:* Wenn du dir nicht sicher bist, ob du ein Verb entweder im Infinitiv belassen sollst oder die Gerundform verwenden musst, probiere beide Möglichkeiten aus und lasse dein Sprachgefühl entscheiden. Wenn du falsch liegst, schreibe die Formulierung in dein Vokabelheft. Achte auch darauf, dass du in manchen Fällen eine Präposition vor dem Gerund benötigst. Mehr Informationen zu diesem Grammatikkapitel findest du auf den Seiten 9 bis 12 in der Kurzgrammatik.

**Two Americans in Stratford-upon-Avon**

Last summer Logan and Andrew, two American students, went on a tour of Europe. Both were looking forward **to spending** a few days in Stratford-upon-Avon. While Logan was keen **on seeing** Shakespeare's birthplace, Andrew wanted **to go** to a performance at the Shakespeare Memorial Theatre.

But they hadn't imagined **being** surrounded by thousands of other tourists. Soon they were not interested **in walking** around the crowded streets anymore and decided **to look** for a place to stay.

But it wasn't easy **to find** a place to sleep. First they went to the tourist information, which was famous **for helping** tourists with their problems. There the nice lady at the desk told them that it was very difficult **to get** a room at that time of the year without **booking** a long time before the holiday. After **phoning** a few hotels, she said there was no place to stay. So she suggested **leaving** Stratford in the evening. The young men were really worried **about finding** a hostel by then, but they did not give up. Finally, they got a small, expensive room in a Bed & Breakfast place about half a mile from the town centre.

**Visiting** Stratford is a fantastic idea, but you must avoid **going** there in the summer.

## III Mediation: Two Americans in Salzburg

*Hinweis:* Wie bei der Mediation üblich, geht es auch hier nicht darum, wortwörtlich zu übersetzen. Einige Informationen passen nicht zu der Jahreszeit (Sommer), in der die beiden Amerikaner nach Salzburg reisen wollen. Beschränke dich also auf das Wesentliche. Für den Inhalt erhältst du 5, für die Sprache 10 Punkte.

In Salzburg, there is a lot to see. They suggest visiting the castle Hohensalzberg because from there you have a great view over the town. It is said to be beautiful, especially in the evening. Then you could walk through the old part of Salzburg and maybe have a look at the house where Mozart was born.

In summer, there are the Festspiele and you can visit concerts, operas and theatre plays. But there are also artists who perform in the streets for free.

Salzburg is known for its sweets: It is recommended to spend some time in one of the cafés and enjoy the "Mozartkugeln" and a cake called "Sachertorte". They offer a lot of different kinds of coffee, too.

You can book places to sleep online: the e-mail address is jugendherbergsnetz @salzburg.at.

(133 words)

**Notenschlüssel:**

| 1 | 2 | 3 | 4 | 5 | 6 |
|---|---|---|---|---|---|
| 46–41 | 40–35 | 34–29 | 28–23 | 22–16 | 15–0 |

## Klassenarbeit 9
**Schwerpunkte:** *Oral exam – Presentation, photo task, role play*

**15–20 minutes**

**I  Presentation: Talking about your hometown** (10 pts.)

Tell us something about your hometown. Talk for about **two minutes** and concentrate on the following aspects:
- information on how to find your hometown in Germany
- interesting facts about your hometown
- places and sights that are worth visiting
- reasons why you like or do not like your hometown

**II  Photo task: Two famous bridges** (20 pts.)

You have got **five minutes'** time to do the following tasks:
1. Look at the two pictures and describe what you can see.
2. Tell us what you know about the two cities the bridges are symbols of.

## III  Role play: A difficult choice (20 pts.)

Read your role card quietly for a minute.
Then start a conversation with your partner. Keep talking for about **five minutes**.

> **Candidate A**
> You are a German pupil on a language course in the south of England and have met a student from France there. You decide to go sightseeing together at the weekend. You would like to go to Brighton.
> Get your friend interested by using the information below or try to reach an agreement.

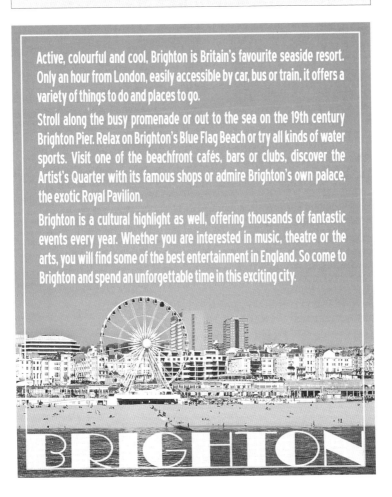

Active, colourful and cool, Brighton is Britain's favourite seaside resort. Only an hour from London, easily accessible by car, bus or train, it offers a variety of things to do and places to go.

Stroll along the busy promenade or out to the sea on the 19th century Brighton Pier. Relax on Brighton's Blue Flag Beach or try all kinds of water sports. Visit one of the beachfront cafés, bars or clubs, discover the Artist's Quarter with its famous shops or admire Brighton's own palace, the exotic Royal Pavilion.

Brighton is a cultural highlight as well, offering thousands of fantastic events every year. Whether you are interested in music, theatre or the arts, you will find some of the best entertainment in England. So come to Brighton and spend an unforgettable time in this exciting city.

**Candidate B**

You are a French pupil on a language course in the south of England and have met a student from Germany there. You decide to go sightseeing together at the weekend. You would like to go to Stonehenge.
Get your friend interested by using the information below or try to reach an agreement.

The site is open from 9 a.m. to 7 p.m. daily (in summer).
Entrance fee: Adult £ 7.50, Child £ 4.50

If you are looking for an unforgettable experience, visit the World Heritage Site of Stonehenge.

The prehistoric monument near the city of Salisbury in Wiltshire is one of the most famous sights of the South West. The stone circle, which was built between 2,500 and 2,000 BC, is surrounded by mystery. Nobody knows if it was a temple, a place to bury the dead or a huge calendar. How did the people in those days manage to carry the huge blocks of stone hundreds of miles by land and water? How did they shape them with primitive tools?

Visitors from all over the world are attracted to this fascinating place. Come to Stonehenge: enjoy the beautiful countryside, see Stonehenge from close up and learn more about its secrets on a guided tour.

# Solution

## I Presentation: Talking about your hometown

> *Hinweis:* Hier solltest du zuerst einige grundlegende Informationen und Sehenswürdigkeiten nennen, dann kannst du beschreiben, was dir persönlich an der Stadt (nicht) gefällt.

I live in Freiburg, a city on the river Rhine in the southwest of Germany. It is only three km from the French border and is famous for its dry, sunny weather in the summer. About 220,000 people live in Freiburg; many of them are students who go to Freiburg University. The university was founded in the 15th century and is one of the best in Germany. Freiburg has got an interesting history, too. You can find many beautiful, old buildings in the city centre, like the famous cathedral, the "Münster", for example.

What I like best about the old part of Freiburg is that there is a large area of the city where no cars are allowed. Freiburg is known as an eco-city and its citizens practised "cycling and recycling" long before other German cities became interested in it.

Freiburg attracts many tourists every year because it offers a great variety of interesting events. There are concerts and wine festivals in the old town in summer and autumn. In the winter you can visit the Christmas market and there is a great carnival celebration in February when people wear colourful costumes and horrible masks and play tricks on the people who watch.

I like living in Freiburg because there are a lot of activities for young people. Many cinemas show the latest films and there are lots of cafés and restaurants where I can meet my friends. If you are interested in sports, you can go ice-skating in the winter and use the swimming pools in the summer. Freiburg is my favourite city.

## II Photo task: Two famous bridges

> *Hinweis:* Betrachte die Bilder genau und erinnere dich an die Regeln für Bildbeschreibungen, die du aus dem Unterricht kennst. Benutze beispielsweise passende Redewendungen wie „In the picture you can see ...", „The picture shows ...", „In the foreground/background, there is/are ...", „on the left/ right ...".

1. The first picture shows Tower Bridge in London. In the foreground you can see the River Thames. Tower Bridge has got two huge towers. When big ships want to pass under it, the traffic across the bridge is stopped and the two parts of the bridge go up. Behind the bridge you can see the skyline of London because Tower Bridge is in the centre of the city.

The second picture shows Harbour Bridge in Sydney, Australia. It is much longer than Tower Bridge and hangs on huge cables. On the left, you can see the Opera House, which is also very famous. You can climb Harbour Bridge with a guide. Harbour Bridge crosses Sydney's harbour so you have got a wonderful view from the top of the bridge.

2. London is the capital of England and the United Kingdom. It is a huge city with almost eight million people. Many of its sights are well-known all over the world, for example the Houses of Parliament and Big Ben, Buckingham Palace, the home of the Queen, Trafalgar Square, Piccadilly Circus and Hyde Park. London is also famous for its many theatres and concert halls, which offer some of the best entertainment in Europe. Visitors like the special atmosphere of London: there are markets, shops and restaurants that sell products from all over the world.

Sydney is smaller than London but it is the biggest city in Australia. About four million people live there. It is famous for the Opera House and its many parks. The Australians are very relaxed people. They believe it is best to have "no worries". A lot of time is spent with going to the beaches around Sydney, having a barbecue and surfing. There are a lot of Asian immigrants in Sydney, but all Australians are immigrants so they welcome the newcomers in a friendly way.

## III Role play: A difficult choice

*Hinweis: Beide Texte enthalten Vokabeln, die dir vielleicht noch nicht bekannt sind, z. B. „World Heritage" (Welterbe). Lies dein Infoblatt genau und versuche, einige Fakten als Argumente für dein Lieblingsausflugsziel im Gespräch zu verwenden. Neben deiner eigenen Sprechfertigkeit solltest du auch die Fähigkeit beweisen, auf deinen Gesprächspartner einzugehen. Es ist also nicht so wichtig, deine Meinung mit allen Mitteln durchzusetzen, sondern vielmehr, das Gespräch in Gang zu halten und zu einer Einigung zu kommen.*

*Beginne das Gespräch am besten mit einer Begrüßungsfloskel, z. B. "How are you?", "How do you do?", „Hey! Any news about ...?"*

*Präge dir zudem vorher einige allgemeine Redewendungen ein, die du in einer Diskussion verwenden kannst, um allzu lange Pausen zu vermeiden.*

- "What do you think?"/„What's your opinion/view (on ...)?"/„How (do you feel) about ...?"/„What do you mean (by ...)?"
- "You're right."/"That's true."/"That's a good idea/point."
- "Are you sure?"/"Do you really think so?"/„I agree, but ..."
- "I don't think so."/„I'm afraid ..."/"I can't agree."
- „Well ..."/„Actually ..."/„The problem is ..."
- „In my opinion/view ..."/„I think/believe ..."

CANDIDATE A: Hi, nice to see you again. How do you like our course so far?

CANDIDATE B: I like it a lot, but I think it's hard work, too, so I'm really looking forward to having some free time now.

CANDIDATE A: Have you already got any plans for the weekend?

CANDIDATE B: Yes, I'd like to do some sightseeing. I've never been to England before and I think there are a lot of interesting places to visit around here.

CANDIDATE A: That's true. Why don't we go on a trip together on Saturday? Let's choose a place we would like to see and find out how we can get there by bus or train.

CANDIDATE B: That's a good idea. So where do you think we should go?

CANDIDATE A: Well, I've heard that Brighton is a great place to visit. I've got a brochure here that says it's "colourful and cool" and there is a lot for young people to do: we could go shopping in the afternoon and in the evening we could go to a play and test our language skills.

CANDIDATE B: Actually I'm more interested in history. I was thinking about going to Stonehenge. Have you heard of it? It's the place everybody goes to in the South of England.

CANDIDATE A: I've heard the name. But what's so special about it?

CANDIDATE B: It's a World Heritage Site, a circle of stones. Nobody knows why it was built and there are a lot of secrets about the place. Some people even believe that it was built by magic because nobody knows how people in those days transported and set up those huge blocks of stone.

CANDIDATE A: Well, that sounds quite interesting. But wouldn't it be better to spend a day on the beach and relax? The brochure says Brighton has got some historical architecture as well. We could visit the Royal Pavilion, a fantastic palace, and walk along the old pier with shops and cafés.

CANDIDATE B: Well, I don't know … Brighton sounds like a lot of fun, but I want to see Stonehenge, too, before I leave.

CANDIDATE A: So why don't you ask the other students? I bet there are some who would like to see Stonehenge as well. And if you don't find anyone else, I promise I'll go with you on Sunday.

CANDIDATE B: OK. So it's Brighton on Saturday and Stonehenge on Sunday. That will be a really exciting weekend!

## Notenschlüssel:

| 1 | 2 | 3 | 4 | 5 | 6 |
|---|---|---|---|---|---|
| 50–45 | 44–39 | 38–32 | 31–25 | 24–16 | 15–0 |

## Klassenarbeit 10
**Schwerpunkte:** *Oral exam – One-minute talk, photo task, role play*

**15–20 minutes**

**I  One-minute talk: Free-time activities** (10 pts.)

Give a short talk about your favourite free-time activity/activities. You have two minutes to prepare your talk. Speak for at least **one minute**. Then you will be asked one or two questions.

**II  Photo task: Cycling in the city** (20 pts.)

You have got **five minutes'** time to do the following tasks:

1. Look at the photo and describe what you can see in it.

2. Imagine you were one of the two girls. Tell the listeners about …
   - where you are.
   - where you want to go.
   - how you feel about riding a bike in the streets of a big city.

## III  Role play: Making plans for the weekend (20 pts.)

Read the role card quietly for a minute.
Then discuss the situation with your partner for about **five minutes**.

> **Candidate A**
>
> You are a 14-year-old teenager. Two of your friends have asked you to spend a weekend with them at a campsite on a nearby lake.
>
> You have always wanted to go camping with your friends and try to persuade your mother/father to let you go.
> Start the conversation by telling your parent about your plans.

> **Candidate B**
>
> You are the mother/father of a 14-year-old teenager. You and your family want to go and see your mother ("Grandma") on Saturday, but your son/daughter has got other plans for the weekend.
>
> Listen to what he/she has got to say and discuss the problem.

**Solution**

## I One-minute talk: Free-time activities

*Hinweis:* Hier solltest du vor allem über ein Hobby sprechen, das dich wirklich interessiert und zu dem du auch auf Englisch einiges erzählen kannst. Ergänze deine Ausführungen durch anschauliche Beispiele. Es ist für die Zuhörer einfacher dir zu folgen, wenn du deine Erzählung etwas strukturierst, also vom Allgemeinen zum Besonderen kommst oder zuerst über die Vorteile und dann über die Nachteile deines bzw. deiner Hobbys sprichst.

I have got a lot of hobbies, but my favourite one is music. I like listening to pop and rock music, especially hard rock. I'm also interested in hip-hop. I often download music from the Internet and listen to it on my iPod. Two years ago my parents bought me an electric guitar and I took some lessons. I've learned a lot since then and I practise almost every day. One night a week two of my friends come to our house and we practise together. I play the guitar and sing, my friends play the bass guitar and the drums. Now we are looking for someone who has got a keyboard and can play quite well because we want to start a real band. We play hard rock and heavy metal – songs by Metallica, Iron Maiden and AC/DC. We haven't got a name for our band yet, but playing together is great fun and I hope we'll soon be able to perform in front of an audience.

Apart from music I like playing football, basketball and table tennis and I often go skiing in the winter. But unfortunately school and homework don't leave me enough time for all the things I would like to do in my free time.

## II Photo task: Cycling in the city

*Hinweis:* Betrachte das Foto, beschreibe es genau und versetze dich in die Rolle eines der beiden Mädchen. Versuche gute Argumente für oder gegen Radfahren in der Großstadt zu finden und schmücke deine Erzählung etwas mit Informationen aus, die näher darauf eingehen, woher ihr kommt, weshalb ihr mit dem Rad unterwegs seid und wie du dich auf dem Fahrrad fühlst.

1. The photo shows a broad street in a big city. In the foreground you can see two girls on a bike. They are crossing the street. The taller girl, who is wearing a white cardigan and dark trousers, is riding the bike. The smaller girl is sitting behind her. Behind the girls, there is a bus stop, traffic signs, posters and a parked car on the right. On the left, several cars are waiting at the traffic lights. In the background you can see city buildings.

2. My friend and I enjoy riding the bike like this very much although it is quite dangerous. One of us might fall off. Still, as we haven't got the money for a monthly ticket for public transport, this is the only way to get to where we want to go quickly. Today, we are meeting some friends from school in the

park. It is quite a long way to walk, so we decided to take the bike. Of course, our parents would never allow us to cycle like that. So we always wait until we're far enough from home and then take off.

## III  Role play: Making plans for the weekend

*Hinweis: Im Rollenspiel müsst ihr hier im Dialog eine Alltagssituation auf Englisch bewältigen. Versuche, dich in deine Rolle zu versetzen und die entsprechenden Argumente zu finden! Nach kurzem „small talk" solltest du bald auf das Problem zu sprechen kommen und versuchen, den Gesprächspartner von deiner Position zu überzeugen. Dabei kommt es nicht darauf an, deine eigene Meinung mit allen Mitteln durchzusetzen, sondern in der Diskussion zu zeigen, dass du auf die Argumente deines Partners eingehen kannst und dich bemühst, zu einer Einigung zu kommen.*

*Damit keine langen Gesprächspausen entstehen, kannst du folgende Füllwörter benutzen:*
- *„OK."/„Well ..."/„I see ..."/„I mean ..."/„Look ..."/„You see ..."*
- *„I'm not sure ..."/„Are you saying that ...?"*

*Um das Gespräch wieder in Gang zu bringen, können diese Formulierungen helfen:*
- *„What do think about ...?"/„Don't you think that ...?"*
- *"I understand what you're saying. But you also have to see that ..."*

CANDIDATE A: Hi, Mum, I'm back from school.

CANDIDATE B: Hi, Max, everything OK?

CANDIDATE A: Yes, of course, the Maths test was quite easy.

CANDIDATE B: Oh good, I'm glad to hear it. Would you like something to drink?

CANDIDATE A: Yes, please, a glass of orange juice would be great ... Mum, can I ask you a question?

CANDIDATE B: Yes, of course, what is it?

CANDIDATE A: Well, you see, Linus and Elias asked me to go camping with them at the weekend. Remember I told you that Elias's uncle and aunt live on a farm near the lake? We can put up the tent in a field and stay there overnight.

CANDIDATE B: But, Max, don't you remember that we promised Grandma to go and see her on Saturday?

CANDIDATE A: Yes, I know, but we see her almost every weekend. So why can't you and Dad go without me this time?

CANDIDATE B: Grandma always likes to see you. You know you are her favourite grandchild and she would be quite sad if you didn't come with us.

CANDIDATE A: But, Mum, I've always wanted to go camping with my friends. And you and Dad promised that I could go some time this summer. So why not go on Saturday? The weather is perfect. I'm sure Grandma will understand.

CANDIDATE B: But you've never been camping before and we haven't even got the necessary equipment.

CANDIDATE A: Linus and Elias can lend me everything I need. It's only for one night. And we aren't far away, so you needn't worry.

CANDIDATE B: Well, it seems you have already organised everything. I think I'll have to agree. But we'll have to ask your dad when he comes home. I don't know what he'll think about it.

CANDIDATE A: Thank you, Mum. I'm sure Dad will say yes, too.

**Notenschlüssel:**

| 1 | 2 | 3 | 4 | 5 | 6 |
|---|---|---|---|---|---|
| 50–45 | 44–39 | 38–32 | 31–25 | 24–16 | 15–0 |

# Ihre Meinung ist uns wichtig!

Ihre Anregungen sind uns immer willkommen. Bitte informieren Sie uns mit diesem Schein über Ihre Verbesserungsvorschläge!

| Titel-Nr. | Seite | Vorschlag |
|---|---|---|
|   |   |   |
|   |   |   |
|   |   |   |
|   |   |   |
|   |   |   |
|   |   |   |
|   |   |   |
|   |   |   |
|   |   |   |
|   |   |   |

Bitte hier abtrennen

Lernen • Wissen • Zukunft
**STARK**

23_V1M

Bitte ausfüllen und im frankierten Umschlag an uns einsenden. Für Fensterkuverts geeignet.

## Zutreffendes bitte ankreuzen!
### Die Absenderin/der Absender ist:

- [ ] Lehrer/in in den Klassenstufen:
- [ ] Fachbetreuer/in
  Fächer:
- [ ] Seminarlehrer/in
  Fächer:
- [ ] Regierungsfachberater/in
  Fächer:
- [ ] Oberstufenbetreuer/in

- [ ] Schulleiter/in
- [ ] Referendar/in, Termin 2. Staatsexamen:
- [ ] Leiter/in Lehrerbibliothek
- [ ] Leiter/in Schülerbibliothek
- [ ] Sekretariat
- [ ] Eltern
- [ ] Schüler/in, Klasse:
- [ ] Sonstiges:

**Unterrichtsfächer:** (Bei Lehrkräften)

**STARK Verlag**
**Postfach 1852**
**85318 Freising**

Kennen Sie Ihre Kundennummer?
Bitte hier eintragen.

### Absender (Bitte in Druckbuchstaben!)

**Name/Vorname**

**Straße/Nr.**

**PLZ/Ort/Ortsteil**

**Telefon privat**          **Geburtsjahr**

**E-Mail**

**Schule/Schulstempel** (Bitte immer angeben!)

Bitte hier abtrennen ✂

# Sicher durch alle Klassen!

Lernerfolg durch selbstständiges Üben zu Hause!
Die von Fachlehrern entwickelten Trainingsbände enthalten alle nötigen Fakten und viele Übungen mit schülergerechten Lösungen.

## Mathematik – Training

| | |
|---|---|
| Mathematik 5. Klasse | Best.-Nr. 90005 |
| Mathematik 5. Klasse – Bayern | Best.-Nr. 900054 |
| Mathematik 6. Klasse | Best.-Nr. 900062 |
| Algebra und Stochastik 7. Klasse | Best.-Nr. 50007 |
| Algebra 7. Klasse – Bayern | Best.-Nr. 900111 |
| Geometrie 7. Klasse – Bayern | Best.-Nr. 900211 |
| Geometrie 7. Klasse | Best.-Nr. 50008 |
| Algebra, Geometrie und Stochastik 8. Klasse – Bayern | Best.-Nr. 900121 |
| Algebra und Stochastik 8. Klasse | Best.-Nr. 50009 |
| Algebra und Stochastik 9. Klasse | Best.-Nr. 900138 |
| Geometrie 9. Klasse | Best.-Nr. 900221 |
| Lineare Gleichungssysteme | Best.-Nr. 900122 |
| Algebra und Stochastik 10. Klasse | Best.-Nr. 900148 |
| Geometrie 10. Klasse | Best.-Nr. 900248 |
| Wiederholung Stochastik | Best.-Nr. 90008 |
| Wiederholung Algebra | Best.-Nr. 90009 |
| Wiederholung Geometrie | Best.-Nr. 90010 |
| Kompakt-Wissen Algebra | Best.-Nr. 90016 |
| Kompakt-Wissen Geometrie | Best.-Nr. 90026 |
| Kompakt-Wissen Grundwissen Algebra · Stochastik · Geometrie – Bayern | Best.-Nr. 900168 📧 |

## Mathematik – Klassenarbeiten · Schulaufgaben

| | |
|---|---|
| Klassenarbeiten Mathematik 5. Klasse | Best.-Nr. 500301 |
| Klassenarbeiten Mathematik 5. Kl. – Bayern | Best.-Nr. 900301 |
| Klassenarbeiten Mathematik 6. Klasse | Best.-Nr. 500302 |
| Schulaufgaben Mathematik 6. Kl. – Bayern | Best.-Nr. 900302 |
| Klassenarbeiten Mathematik 7. Klasse | Best.-Nr. 500311 |
| Schulaufgaben Mathematik 7. Kl. – Bayern | Best.-Nr. 900311 |
| Klassenarbeiten Mathematik 8. Klasse | Best.-Nr. 500321 |
| Schulaufgaben Mathematik 8. Kl. – Bayern | Best.-Nr. 900321 |
| Klassenarbeiten Mathematik 9. Klasse | Best.-Nr. 500331 |
| Schulaufgaben Mathematik 9. Kl. – Bayern | Best.-Nr. 900331 |
| Klassenarbeiten Mathematik 10. Klasse | Best.-Nr. 900341 |

## Mathematik – STARK in Klassenarbeiten

| | |
|---|---|
| Brüche und Dezimalzahlen 5.–8. Klasse | Best.-Nr. 900065 |
| Prozentrechnen 6.–8. Klasse | Best.-Nr. 900063 |
| Potenzen und Potenzfunktionen 5.–10. Klasse | Best.-Nr. 900066 |

## Chemie/Biologie

| | |
|---|---|
| Chemie – Mittelstufe 1 | Best.-Nr. 90731 📧 |
| Chemie – Mittelstufe 2 | Best.-Nr. 90732 📧 |
| Kompakt-Wissen Grundwissen Chemie | Best.-Nr. 907301 📧 |
| Training Biologie – Unterstufe | Best.-Nr. 90701 📧 |
| Training Biologie – Mittelstufe 1 | Best.-Nr. 90702 |
| Training Biologie – Mittelstufe 2 | Best.-Nr. 90703 |
| Kompakt-Wissen Biologie Unter- und Mittelstufe | Best.-Nr. 907001 |

## Physik

| | |
|---|---|
| Physik – Mittelstufe 1 | Best.-Nr. 90301 📧 |
| Physik – Mittelstufe 2 | Best.-Nr. 90302 📧 |
| Physik – Übertritt in die Oberstufe | Best.-Nr. 80301 |

## Geschichte

| | |
|---|---|
| Kompakt-Wissen Geschichte Unter-/Mittelstufe | Best.-Nr. 907601 |

## Deutsch – Training

| | |
|---|---|
| Rechtschreibung und Diktat 5./6. Kl. mit CD | Best.-Nr. 90408 |
| Aufsatz 5./6. Klasse | Best.-Nr. 90401 |
| Leseverstehen 5./6. Klasse | Best.-Nr. 90410 |
| Grammatik und Stil 5./6. Klasse | Best.-Nr. 90406 |
| Zeichensetzung 5.–7. Klasse | Best.-Nr. 944013 |
| Leseverstehen 7./8. Klasse | Best.-Nr. 90411 |
| Grammatik und Stil 7./8. Klasse | Best.-Nr. 90407 |
| Aufsatz 7./8. Klasse | Best.-Nr. 90403 |
| Aufsatz 9./10. Klasse | Best.-Nr. 90404 |
| Diktat 5.–10. Klasse mit MP3-CD | Best.-Nr. 944012 |
| Deutsche Rechtschreibung 5.–10. Klasse | Best.-Nr. 944011 |
| Übertritt in die Oberstufe | Best.-Nr. 90409 |
| Kompakt-Wissen Rechtschreibung | Best.-Nr. 944065 📧 |
| Kompakt-Wissen Deutsch Aufsatz Unter-/Mittelstufe | Best.-Nr. 904401 |
| Grundwissen Epochen der deutschen Literatur im Überblick | Best.-Nr. 104401 |

## Deutsch – Klassenarbeiten

| | |
|---|---|
| Klassenarbeiten 5. Klasse | Best.-Nr. 104051 |
| Klassenarbeiten 6. Klasse | Best.-Nr. 104061 |
| Klassenarbeiten 7. Klasse | Best.-Nr. 104071 |
| Klassenarbeiten 8. Klasse | Best.-Nr. 104081 |
| Klassenarbeiten 9. Klasse | Best.-Nr. 104091 |

## Deutsch – STARK in Klassenarbeiten

| | |
|---|---|
| Argumentieren 7./8. Klasse | Best.-Nr. 90414 |
| Erörtern 9./10. Klasse | Best.-Nr. 90413 |
| Gedichtanalyse 9./10. Klasse | Best.-Nr. 90412 |

 Alle so gekennzeichneten Titel sind auch als eBook über **www.stark-verlag.de** erhältlich.

*(Bitte blättern Sie um)*

## Englisch Grundwissen

Englisch 5. Klasse mit MP3-CD
Lesen · Schreiben · Hören · Wortschatz ........... Best.-Nr. 90516
Englisch Grammatik 5. Klasse ........................ Best.-Nr. 90505
Englisch 6 Klasse mit MP3-CD
Lesen · Schreiben · Hören · Wortschatz ........... Best.-Nr. 90533
Englisch Grammatik 6. Klasse ........................ Best.-Nr. 90506
Englisch Grammatik 7. Klasse ........................ Best.-Nr. 90507
Hörverstehen 7. Klasse mit CD ...................... Best.-Nr. 90513
Englisch Grammatik 8. Klasse ........................ Best.-Nr. 90508
Leseverstehen 8. Klasse ................................ Best.-Nr. 90522
Englisch Grammatik 9. Klasse ........................ Best.-Nr. 90509
Englisch Grammatik 10. Klasse ...................... Best.-Nr. 90510
Textproduktion 9./10. Klasse ........................ Best.-Nr. 90541
Wortschatzübung Mittelstufe ........................ Best.-Nr. 90520
Englisch Übertritt in die Oberstufe ................ Best.-Nr 82453

## Englisch – Klassenarbeiten

Klassenarbeiten Englisch 5. Kl. mit Audio-CD ... Best.-Nr. 905053
Klassenarbeiten Englisch 6. Kl. mit Audio-CD ... Best.-Nr. 905063
Klassenarbeiten Englisch 7. Kl. mit Audio-CD ... Best.-Nr. 905073
Klassenarbeiten Englisch 8. Kl. mit MP3-CD ... Best.-Nr. 104681
Klassenarbeiten Englisch 9. Kl. mit MP3-CD ... Best.-Nr. 105093
Klassenarbeiten Englisch 10. Kl. mit MP3-CD ... Best.-Nr. 104611

## Englisch Kompakt-Wissen

Kompakt-Wissen Kurzgrammatik ................. Best.-Nr. 90461
Kompakt-Wissen Grundwortschatz ............... Best.-Nr. 90464

## Sprachenzertifikat · DELF

Sprachenzertifikat Englisch Niveau A 2
mit Audio-CD ............................................... Best.-Nr. 105552
Sprachenzertifikat Englisch Niveau B 1
mit Audio-CD ............................................... Best.-Nr. 105550
Sprachenzertifikat Französisch
DELF B1 mit MP3-CD ..................................... Best.-Nr. 105530

## Französisch

Französisch im 1. Lernjahr ............................ Best.-Nr. 905502
Rechtschreibung und Diktat 1./2. Lernjahr
mit 2 CDs ..................................................... Best.-Nr. 905501
Französisch im 2. Lernjahr ............................ Best.-Nr. 905503
Französisch im 3. Lernjahr ............................ Best.-Nr. 905504
Französisch im 4. Lernjahr ............................ Best.-Nr. 905505
Wortschatzübung Mittelstufe ........................ Best.-Nr. 94510
Kompakt-Wissen Grundwortschatz ............... Best.-Nr. 905001

## Latein

Latein I/II im 1. Lernjahr 5./6. Klasse ........... Best.-Nr. 906051
Latein I/II im 2. Lernjahr 6./7. Klasse ........... Best.-Nr. 906061
Latein I/II im 3. Lernjahr 7./8. Klasse ........... Best.-Nr. 906071
Übersetzung im 1. Lektürejahr ..................... Best.-Nr. 906091
Übersetzung im 2. Lektürejahr ..................... Best.-Nr. 906092
Wiederholung Grammatik ............................ Best.-Nr. 94601
Wortkunde ................................................... Best.-Nr. 94603
Kompakt-Wissen Kurzgrammatik .................. Best.-Nr. 906011
Kompakt-Wissen
Sachwissen zum Lateinunterricht .................. Best.-Nr. 906012

## Spanisch

Spanisch im 1. Lernjahr ................................ Best.-Nr. 905401
Spanisch im 2. Lernjahr ................................ Best.-Nr. 905402
Kompakt-Wissen Grundwortschatz ............... Best.-Nr. 945402

 Alle so gekennzeichneten Titel sind auch als eBook
über **www.stark-verlag.de** erhältlich.

**Natürlich führen wir noch mehr Titel für alle
Fächer und Stufen: Alle Informationen unter
www.stark-verlag.de**

**Bestellungen bitte direkt an:**
STARK Verlagsgesellschaft mbH & Co. KG · Postfach 1852 · 85318 Freising
Tel. 0180 3 179000* · Fax 0180 3 179001* · www.stark-verlag.de · info@stark-verlag.de
*9 Cent pro Min. aus dem deutschen Festnetz, Mobilfunk bis 42 Cent pro Min.
Aus dem Mobilfunknetz wählen Sie die Festnetznummer: 08167 9573-0

Lernen · Wissen · Zukunft